CONCILIUM

Religion in the Seventies

CONCILIUM

Editorial Directors

Concilium 116 (6/1978): Project X

BUDDHISM AND CHRISTIANITY

Edited by
Claude Geffré
and
Mariasusai Dhavamony

A CROSSROAD BOOK
The Seabury Press • New York

1979
The Seabury Press
815 Second Avenue
New York, N.Y. 10017

Library of Congress Catalog Card Number: 78-71625
ISBN: 0-8164-0395-3
ISBN: 0-8164-2612-0 (pbk.)
Printed in the United States of America

CONTENTS

Part III
Bulletins

Editorial

THE UNITY of mankind and the creation of one world are the great ideals of modern man. Recent times have witnessed a widening of horizons, a crumbling of dividing frontiers, and a drawing together of peoples once far apart. This trend is thrown into high relief by the far-reaching change that equally affects East and West. As far as the West is concerned, a silent but effective influence of eastern religions, especially Buddhism, has taken place. Here is a vital challenge for every Christian either to accept the religio-moral values of Buddhism and to enrich his own religious outlook, or to pretend that nothing valuable exists in it and to even erect a defence against it. The problem arises not only with respect to the West but more especially with the Christians who live among Buddhists in Asia. The spirit of openness initiated by Vatican II demands that we should respect and preserve whatever is holy and true in other religious traditions, and enter into dialogue and co-operate with their followers without omitting our own witness to Christ. (*Nostra Aetate,* n. 2) This call for inter-religious dialogue was largely unknown before the Council.

Extending itself over so many vast culture areas of South and East Asia, Buddhism has exercised a powerful influence over the thinking and life of millions of peoples and has established a greater universality than any other Asian religion. The purpose of this *Concilium* is not so much to give a complete account of Buddhism as found in various countries of Asia and elsewhere, and to treat exhaustively all aspects of Buddhist-Christian dialogue, as to allow specialists to explain the mainstream of Buddhist thought and practice. This will, we hope, aid inter-faith understanding and raise the theological problems involved in Buddhist-Christian dialogue, rather than solve them.

We approach Buddhism from the religious standpoint, with a concept of religion largely based on historico-phenomenological studies and yet with genuine eagerness to understand Buddhism in terms of its own traditions, as it is lived by its followers, and what has been most deeply meaningful in their religious precept and practice.

But can I, as a Christian, really understand Buddhism? Some hold that religions are understandable only to those who adhere to them; namely, that every religion is understandable only if one believes in it, for each religion reveals its proper inner meaning only to its believers.

But there certainly is a difference between 'understanding' and 'believing'; it is not true that we cannot understand another religion unless we believe ourselves in it, and thus 'enter' into it. 'To believe' means to accept the truths which a religion proposes as definitive and in some sense ultimate, and to be so convinced of those truths as to live by them. 'To understand' means to grasp the meaning of a fact or phenomenon by the manifestation of this phenomenon. Now we can understand a religious phenomenon only through its manifestation in symbols: language, ritual, and gestures. Inner experience finds its expression in a language: in prayer, myths, revelations; in an action: in ritual and in gestures; both are complementary and give us the total meaning and significance of the religious phenomenon. Such a religious expression is given us by the believers of each religion themselves. A member of one faith can understand the meaning of another faith in so far as he or she perceives it through respect, personal contact and empathy, and grasp to some extent the inner meaning of another's faith. So is the interfaith understanding between Christianity and Buddhism.

Sometimes we come across the inability of the two faiths, in particular, Christianity and Buddhism, to communicate at crucial points. Even Christians of a particular nation find themselves in a similar predicament when they try to communicate themselves and their Christian faith to their Buddhist fellow countrymen. Very often they feel that they are walking on parallel tracks without meeting. Given the difficulties and hardships of interfaith dialogue, we simply cannot assume that interfaith dialogue is impossible and that one cannot really understand another faith unless one truly believes in it. On this supposition we have to conclude that either the dialogue tends to portray the eternal and absolute separation of the two faiths, or—particularly in the East—that it tends to accept uncritically the immediate syncretism or the discovery that both beliefs are at bottom identical. We have to avoid these attempts at extremes in the interest of some sort of genuine dialogue. Both Buddhism and Christianity are radically different and at the same time radically similar; neither one alone nor the other alone. Dialogue will be impossible at either extreme of radical discontinuity between or radical oneness of the two faiths. For a fruitful dialogue there must be a proper sense of difference and likeness.

Buddhism presents itself as a way of salvation or deliverance from oneself and from the world; as an answer to man's desperate condition, to one caught unceasingly in a succession of lives whose main characteristics are suffering, impermanence, and unreality; and as possessing an infallible technique for freeing man from such a situation of bondage. This has been taught and lived by the Buddha himself, showing the way to *nirvāna*, the state of absolute, immutable bliss, free of suffering and woe.

In this *Concilium* we have decided to select the central teaching of Buddhism on deliverance and hence offer studies describing the significance and meaning of deliverance and the ways of achieving such a goal.

A keen awareness of suffering without any delusion about it forms the basis of Buddhism. The Buddha's insight is concentrated in the four noble truths: the existence of suffering, the causes of suffering, the cessation of suffering, and the path that leads to the cessation of suffering. Buddha's teaching was realistic; by penetrating the causes of suffering, he showed how suffering could be eradicated. The word 'suffering' has far greater depth and complexity than 'pain', 'grief', 'misery'; it refers to impermanence, emptiness and lack of perfection. Suffering can be experienced at three levels. First, there is suffering inherent in the life-process itself, in birth, old age, sickness, death, and all other accidents to which life is subject. Second, there is the suffering of sentient, conscious creatures who know the gap between desire and realization, and are aware of the transient nature of all things. Third, suffering arises out of the actual nature and constitution of human beings.

The plan of the argument has three parts. In the first we take into consideration the experience of suffering and of liberation. The fact of suffering and of human condition in Buddhism includes the following problems. What is suffering *(dukkha)* according to the Buddhists? The fact of suffering supplies the main impulse of Buddhist thinking to analyze suffering and the quest for liberation from it, both of which constitute the main contents of the quest. The cycle of rebirth *(saṁsāra)* and the law of action *(kamma)*, craving *(taṇhā)* in the form of greed *(lobha)*, hatred *(dosa)* and delusion *(moha)* are the root causes of suffering. Suffering is understood as pain, misery and grief: suffering is inherent in the life-process, as a gap between what one desires and what one possesses, as an aggregate of existence itself, and as the actual nature of man.

What are the paths or ways of liberation that Buddhism proposes to solve the problem of suffering and delusion or ignorance? Faith *(saddhā)* as confidence in the three jewels and deliverance is the first requisite. Moral path *(sīla)* consists in the practice of virtues, especially of non-injury. This is followed by the paths of concentration *(samādhi)* and that of wisdom *(paññā)*. Deliverance is conceived of as a type of experience that strives for the acquisition of an unconditioned state *(asaṁskṛta)* which is an escape from the concatenation of causes, and consequently from sorrow; it implies the cessation of all desires and of all becoming, a neutralization of acts; and finally it is the intuitive realization of the Buddha nature and Buddha wisdom. Various types of deliverance *(nibbāna)* are described. To partake of the Buddha nature means not only to share in the timeless bliss of nibbana but also to have a part in the Buddha's own boundless wisdom, compassion and love.

Theological perspectives raise many problems such as the following. What is the principal obstacle to fruitful dialogue between Buddhism and Christianity? What is the probable best method of approach in dialogue? Experience of suffering and of impermanence, experience of non-injury and compassion, experience of liberation and its ways can be compared to the analogous Christian experience of these facts. While attending to the convergence and divergence of the two religious experiences, stress should be put on the rich values of meditation, the spirit of detachment, and the spirit of love and compassion so highly valued in Buddhism. A keen sense of suffering and impermanence, respect for life and the realization of the state of non-suffering, freedom, and peace are positive values of Buddhism which can enrich Christian experience. How far can this enrichment take place within Christian tradition and spirituality? What can Buddhism contribute to a deeper experience of Christ? How should we present Christ to Buddhists? A theological evaluation of the Buddha and of his mission is also interesting.

In this context it should be noted that the theological evaluation of another religious tradition (here, of Buddhism) by a Christian takes place in the light of Christian revelation and faith. This precisely is the rôle and function of the theology of world religions, for theology makes use of the criteria of Christian revelation and faith in judging the claims of other religious traditions when they propose and realize the ways and means of human salvation. Finally, the bulletins are by four specialists who have spent many years in Buddhist countries and have rich experience of Buddhist-Christian dialogue; they outline the dialogical situation and its problems and difficulties in Sri Lanka, Thailand, Cambodia, Burma, Malaysia, Laos and Japan. There is also a report on the influence of Buddhism in Europe and America.

MARIASUSAI DHAVAMONY
CLAUDE GEFFRÉ

PART I

The Experience of Suffering and of Liberation

Andre Bareau

The Experience of Suffering and the Human Condition in Buddhism

ACCORDING to all the canonical texts, irrespective of the sect, Buddhism has always been a method of saving beings, and especially men, and of releasing them finally from the suffering inherent in any existence, and then leading them to a state of unutterable and everlasting blessedness, outside the unending cycle of rebirths (*samsara*).

It relies therefore on two propositions: one is a belief of the Indians among whom it originated; the other is the result of the personal experience and meditation of the founder, Gautama, known as the Buddha: that is, 'he who was awakened to truth'. The first of these two postulates suggests that every living being will be reborn an infinite number of times after his death, just as he lived an incalculable number of lives in the past. The second says that every life is of its nature hard and full of deception and pain. That is true not only of the damned in hell, the starving and wandering revenants and animals that are subject to fear, hunger and a thousand other torments, but of men who are spared neither punishment nor suffering. As for gods and spirits of all kinds, their existence is very long and quite pleasant, but must come to an end after which they will be reborn, usually among other classes of being who lead a harsh life.

A well-known legend offers a traditional explanation of the origin of Buddhism. Gautama, the future Buddha, was a young prince living a rich and pleasurable life. His father the king had taken care that his son should not even suspect the existence of any suffering or pain. But in the course of three walks the young man came upon a sick man, an old man and a dead body—one after the other. Hence he encountered three most striking manifestations of pain and suffering. He learned from his adviser that such was the inescapable fate of all men, including himself. The young prince was greatly affected. He was sad and troubled. Not long after, during another stroll, he saw an ascetic whose calm expression was so impressive that a few hours later Gautama left his palace to lead the wandering life of a religious beggar. After years of austerity and profound meditation, he reached the point of awakening or illumination (*bodhi*), that is, the discovery of truth and salvation, and thus founded Buddhism.[1]

It is certain that the future Buddha was not this rich young prince who knew no hardship, but that as a young man he was a rough-living warrior belonging to a minor frontier tribe in a hostile area with few resources, always open to many serious dangers, to scarcity and sickness, to accidents while hunting and to the rigours of war. From childhood he knew all the hardship of the human condition and, like his young companions, or even better than them, he endured and thus forged that noble and forceful character which he was to demonstrate so often later on. The spiritual event which made him decide, shortly after the birth of his son Rahula, to leave his family, friends and way of life forever in order to become a wandering ascetic must have been especially harsh, but tradition has lost all memory of it and we are reduced to mere conjecture on this major aspect of the history of Buddhism. Only the sudden death of someone very dear to him could, it seems, explain so sudden and complete a change of life.[2]

Whatever this decisive experience of the young Gautama was, it is certain that he found it very painful and that is formed not only the basis of his meditation but the fundamentals of his teaching; it posed a problem, and he searched for a solution for a long time until he found it. Everything would seem to show that, during the years between his flight and this discovery, he was obsessed by the memory of this terrible event. The proof is that pain is the subject-matter of the first of the four truths (*satya, sacca*)[3] whose sudden manifestation constituted what is called 'awakening' (*bodhi*).

'Everything is suffering: birth is suffering, sickness is suffering, old age is suffering, death is suffering, union with a person one does not love is suffering, separation from the one whom one loves is suffering, not to obtain what one desires is suffering, the five aggregates of appropriation (which make up the person) are suffering'—that is what the sage Gautama (now the Buddha) taught, shortly after his awakening, to his first five disciples, in the Antelope Park near Benares.[4]

The word that we translate as 'suffering' or 'pain', *duḥkha* in Sanskrit, *dukka* in Pāli, has a very broad meaning, much more extensive than the English words used to translate it. It stands for everything displeasing, from the slightest annoyance to the most awful suffering, both physical and mental pain, a difficulty, and unhappiness and despair. It is used both as an adjective and as a noun, so that the first truth reads: 'Everything is painful, and harsh . . .' if we do not take the context and commentaries as allowing us to translate as already suggested.

The Buddha and his first disciples developed this idea in many sermons: Everything in existence is painful, from birth to death. It is pointless to cite all the pleasures and joys resulting from the satisfaction of the senses and the mind, which are the main goals of human action. All these pleasures and joys are deceptive, ephemeral, fleeting, often mixed with disagreeable or bitter impressions, and especially the fear that they will cease sooner or later. Hence the true nature of the existence of all living beings is essentially deceptive, sad and painful. Behind this pessimistic notion of life there is not only the memory of the tragic event which persuaded Gautama to leave lay life in order to become a wandering ascetic beggar, but that of the hard conditions in which he had passed his youth. This was a memory which must very often have nourished his meditations and in some way 'crystallized' about that of the tragic event that had shaken his life. Long experience of more than twenty years in the forests of the Teraï showed him that dangers, fears, deceptions, hunger, thirst, illness, accidents, setbacks, sorrow and affliction are the stuff of life, that pleasures and joys are rare and transient, and that their cessation makes life all the harder.

Is it possible to avoid pain, and what it does to life? That is the problem that the future Buddha tried to resolve after coming to his sad conclusion. There was no point in bringing death nearer, or in waiting patiently for it, because another birth and another existence would soon follow the end of the present life, according to the Indian beliefs which Gautama did not doubt.

To discover the desired means of salvation, it was necessary first to know the causes of pain and, more generally, the causes of existence which is so closely linked to suffering. The meditations of the sage Gautama revealed three causes: actions, thirst or fierce longing, and ignorance of reality.

He first arrived at the conviction that creatures were reborn according to their actions (karman, kamma), in the sense that those who had committed bad actions through the body, voice or mind would return after dying the 'bad fate' (durgati) of the damned, as animals, hungry revenants, or men burdened by all kinds of hardship, whereas those who had performed good actions would be reborn into 'good fates' (sugati) as gods or men living lives without hardship, in good health and with other advantages.[5] It would seem that this idea was borrowed by the future Buddha from earlier Indian thinkers, but even then Gautama deserves praise for having made it one of the main bases of his teaching and for having given it a high moral value. It is as a result of this belief that the suppression or total 'exhaustion' of the passions and the cultivation of the virtues, of methods tending to weaken and then destroy the first, and of those which are intended to develop the second, enjoy a major place in Buddhism.

The other causes would seem to have been discovered by Gautama himself during the famous night of illumination, or shortly afterwards. The first, defined as the origin (*samudaya*) of suffering, is 'thirst' (*tṛṣṇā, taṇhā*): that is, ardent desire, as demanding as the thirst suffered by inhabitants of tropical countries like India. It is the object of the second of the four truths taught by the Buddha in his famous Benares sermon. It is thirst which brings about rebirth, a return to existence. Being intrinsically linked to the desire for all kinds of pleasures, it is satisfied here and there, and drives the creature to be reborn again and again in order to enjoy those pleasures unceasingly. That is why it is also and above all an ardent desire for life, and therefore to be reborn, and why it is the cause of existences and, consequently, of suffering.[6]

Under different names, sensual desire (*kāma*) or covetousness (*lobha*), it is often denounced in Buddha's sermons, together with hatred (*dveṣa, dosa*) and deviation, error or stupidity (*moha*), as comprising the three 'roots of evil' (*akusalamūla*), that is, the three basic vices from which all others derive. In fact, hatred and similar passions, anger, malice, and so on, may be thought of as manifestations of a certain form of desire: the desire for the disappearance of displeasing objects or creatures; that is why they are never described as being direct causes of suffering or (the same thing) of existence.

On the contrary, deviation, under the name of ignorance (*avidyā, avijjā*), is given in the famous statement of the law of 'conditional production' (*pratītyasamutpāda, paṭiccasamuppāda*)—discovered by the Buddha shortly after awakening—as the prime origin of suffering, existence, and all that is. Ignorance is the first of the twelve links of the chain of twelve conditions, each link having as a condition of production (*pratītya, paṭicca*) that which precedes it, and conditioning the appearance of that which follows it. Thirst (*tṛṣṇā, taṇhā*) is the eighth, having as its direct cause sensation (*vedanā*), and as a direct consequence appropriation (*upadāna*). From this is born existence (*bhava*), whence also come birth (*jāti*), death (*maraṇā*) and the various forms of suffering, disappointment, regret, sadness, and torment. It is this ignorance which prevents one from knowing the reality discovered by the Buddha: that is, the four truths (*satya/sacca*) concerning suffering, its origin, its cessation and the way which leads to the last. By means of the illusions it creates, and especially the pleasing objects of sensations, vain and deceptive phenomena, it causes the appearance of ardent desire, which brings about rebirth and perhaps suffering. It is ignorance which constructs the trap in which creatures are caught and from which they can never escape.[7]

In addition to suffering directly caused by a painful sensation or a painful thought, Buddhism has always acknowledged the existence of pain and suffering arising indirectly from the illusory and deceptive nature of pleasures and other objects of desire. All pleasures and joys are transient and often fleeting, and their cessation produces the sadness of deception, frustration and regret. That is so because the creature, and man especially, is unaware that everything and everyone are subject to the inexorable law of impermanence (*anityatā, aniccatā*); that everything is restricted in time and in space; that everything has a beginning and will have an end; that nothing is everlasting; and that everything changes, more or less quickly but assuredly, between the moment of its appearance and that of its disappearance. The thing one wanted degrades and then is destroyed: the flower one admired withers, then turns to dust; the creature that one loved grows old and then dies. If everything is impermanent, changing, transitory, it is because everything is made up (*saṃskṛta, saṅkhata*) of multiple and diverse, mental or material elements (*dhātu*), which are themselves only phenomena without consistency or duration, giving rise to or conditioning one another, forming among themselves very complex combinations which are constantly renewed; it is because, in the midst of all that, there is nothing unchanging or eternal, nothing which is uncreated and therefore indestructible. There is nothing perfectly pure and simple in the thing or being which one looks on, desires, loves or enjoys; that is because everything is subject to the great universal law of the absence of 'self' (*anātman, anattä*), that is, of a personal, immutable and eternal principle.

To use an expression which appeared at the start of Buddhism, and which has been used to designate its entire metaphysics, 'everything is empty' (*śūnya, suñña*), empty of 'self', empty of its own nature, empty of what Christians call the soul; it is here that Buddhist philosophy differs essentially from that of Brahmanism, which affirms the existence of the individual 'self' and of the universal 'self', of *ātman* and *brahman*, which are consubstantial with one another. The Buddhist 'emptiness' is not nothingness, but something very subtle on the borderline between being and nothingness, something which the ideas of modern physics allow us to glimpse in the immense spaces separating the infinitesimal particles comprising matter, even the most solid, and in those impalpable waves which determine all the properties of matter:

its colours, heat, light, sound, and so on. Though we should not follow certain excessive enthusiasts in concluding that, thanks to his extraordinary wisdom, the Buddha was aware of the science of our own times twenty-five centuries beforehand, we should acknowledge the non-convergence of ideas of the world and things in it, which are very different to what they seem to be when presented to our senses and to our mind, especially in the case of the matter which the mind believes and grasps at, which is then shown to be no more than an illusion resulting from our imperfect means of cognition. The objects of human desires (which condition most of our activities) are therefore no more than shadows, and not solid and lasting creatures such as we tend to think them to be; this difference between reality and appearance is one of the main causes of distress and suffering because of the deceptions it evokes.

Moreover, man is himself one of these shades without any consistency, a collection of material phenomena, sensations, percepts, various mental phenomena and aspects of consciousness, which change incessantly, to such an extent that he constantly changes between his birth and his death even though he imagines that he is always the same. Consequently his tastes and his desires change with him; and then the object which he desired so ardently, and which he enjoyed for a time, abandons him and becomes yet another source of distress. Hence the inconsistent and unstable nature of the subject of desire combines with the analogous nature of the object of desire and produces pain and suffering.

One of the best illustrations of this truth is the famous scene which, in the legend of the future Buddha, immediately precedes and becomes the direct cause of his flight. Worried by the four meetings, the young prince passes the night in his harem, where his concubines, chosen from among the most beautiful and attractive of women, try to distract him by singing, dancing and playing musical instruments. Gautama goes to sleep and the women soon follow him. During the night the prince wakes up and, seeing the bodies of the dancers and musicians given up to sleep but lying in various states of disarray, with their jewelry disarranged, groaning, grinding their teeth, snoring, and quite without appeal, he suddenly thinks in horror that he has woken up in a vault full of dead people. Overcome by disgust and horror, he decides to leave at once. He awakens his groom, has his horse saddled and gallops off into the night, not stopping until dawn, far from the city where his family and acquaintances are still asleep.[8]

The concubines whose beauty had once so attracted him had certainly lost some of their appeal, but it is the transformation of his mind and spirit, violently struck by the revelations of the four previous encounters, which had made these women seem so very dreadful. Although this story is of course purely legendary, there is no point where its verisimilitude can be faulted. Its psychological truth is incontestable, and history offers supporting evidence which there is no reason to doubt.

The contrast between the two successive scenes makes this legend a very striking illustration of the truth of suffering, and therefore of the extremely pessimistic idea which the Buddha and his disciples had of existence, and of the ephemeral and deceptive because illusory nature of the objects of desire and of the pleasures they afford. However sharp and attractive those objects and their pleasures are, they soon give rise to satiation, indifference and disgust, and even horror or hatred, if not frustration or regret. The wise man should not allow himself to be caught in their traps but look courageously and directly at the reality of the intrinsically painful and distressing nature of existence. That is the first lesson which the Buddha teaches men, and the first step on the long road to liberation.

Translated by John Griffiths

Notes

1. This legend was told for the first time in the *Mahāpadāna-sutta*, *sutta* No. 1414 of the *Dīgha-nikāya pāli*, and its Sanskrit and Chinese analogues. There it is also told of a mythical predecessor of Gautama, the Buddha Vipassin, but it is also said that it applies to all Buddhas, and therefore to Gautama. It reappears in the post-canonical biographies of Gautama.

2. See A. Bareau, 'La jeunesse du Buddha dans les *Sūtra-piṭaka* et *Vinaya-piṭaka* anciens', in *Bulletin de l'Ecole française d'Extrême-Orient*, 61 (1974), pp. 199-274, especially the end.

3. When the orthography of the Indian word is the same in Sanskrit and in Pāli, only one word appears; when two appear, the first is Sanskrit, the second Pāli.

4. See the Pāli *Dhammacakkappavattana-sutta* of the *Saṃyuttanikāya*, vol. V, pp. 420 ff., and its Sanskrit and Chinese analogues.

5. See the *Bhayabherava-sutta* and the *Dvedhāvitakka-sutta*, sutta Nos. 4 and 19 of the *Majjhima-nikāya* in Pāli and their Sanskrit and Chinese analogues.

6. See the *Dhammacakkappavattana-sutta* of the *Saṃyuttanikāya* in Pāli, vol. V, pp. 420 ff. and their Sanskrit and Chinese analogues.

7. See the *Mahā-vagga* of the Pāli *Vinaya-piṭaka*, v. 1. I, pp. 1, 2 and its Sanskrit and Chinese analogues.

8. The oldest version of this legend which we have retained is to be found in the Chinese translation of the *Vinaya-piṭaka* of the Mahiśāsaka, No. 1421 of the Taishô Issaikyô edition of the Chinese Buddhist canon, p. 102a. A quite similar story, but applied to Yasa, one of the first disciples of the Buddha, is given in the *Mahā-vagga* of the *Vinaya-piṭaka* in Pāli, Vol. I, pp. 15, 16, and its Sanskrit and Chinese analogues.

James W. Boyd

The Path of Liberation from Suffering in Buddhism

THE BUDDHIST Path of Liberation from suffering is a contemplative one. It is three-fold in its emphasis, involving the practice of morality (*sīla*), concentration meditation (*sāmadhi*), and insight meditation or wisdom (*paññā*). An important formulation of this integrated contemplative path is found in the work of Buddhaghosa of the fifth century, AD. Buddhaghosa's encyclopaedic work, the *Path of Purification* (*Visuddhimagga*),[1] is a digest of the entire Theravadin canonical scriptures and their Sinhalese commentaries and provided the standard schematization of the Path which formed Mahayana practices in China and Tibet and which persists in the Theravadin tradition today.

MORALITY (*SĪLA*)

When referring to morality, one normally thinks of virtuous conduct. This is also the initial connotation of the Buddhist term *sīla* (morality, virtue). However, there is another dimension to the Buddhist concept of morality which is not readily conveyed by the notion of virtuous conduct. According to Buddhaghosa, the nature of moral activity must be understood as basically involving mental formations which give rise to certain types of mental, verbal and bodily actions. According to Buddhist analysis, there are fifty-two possible conditions accompanying any conscious moment which, taken together, form a particular mental formation (B.XIV.131ff.). For example, among the fifty-two attendant conditions of consciousness (*cetasika*), contact, volition and attention are invariably present in any active conscious moment. Other accompanying conditions, such as sustained thought and resolutions,

11

are only sometimes present. If it is a profitable moment of consciousness (that is, results in good *kamma*), the concomitants of mindfulness, faith, non-greed and tranquillity will invariably be present. Unprofitable, unvirtuous mental formations, on the other hand, will necessarily include delusion and agitation, and likely wrong views, conceit (pride), envy and uncertainty.

Virtuous actions, therefore, are initially profitable mental formations which include feelings and perceptions as attendant conditions. A person who abstains from killing living beings, does not take what is not given, and avoids sexual misconduct, performs these virtuous bodily actions on the basis of a virtuous mental foundation. Likewise, the profitable composition (B.I.19) of various mental formations results in virtuous verbal acts such as abstention from false, malicious or harsh speech and gossip, or forms the virtuous mental states which avoid covetousness, ill-will and wrong views (B.I.140). Virtue is also present in one who possesses the seven good states: faith, conscience, fear of wrong-doing, learning, energy, mindfulness and understanding. An eighth type of profitable state is right livelihood. Whoever avoids unprofitable mental foundations avoids the consequent impure acts, and whoever establishes himself in positive mental states, like faith and mindfulness, performs virtuous acts. The importance of mindfulness will become clearer when we discuss the meaning of the two other major components of the Buddhist Path, namely concentration (*samādhi*) and wisdom (*paññā*). A clarification of the meaning of faith in the Buddhist context is, however, appropriate at this point.

Faith (*saddhā*) refers to the contemplative's confidence in the witness of the Buddha, his teachings (*Dhamma*) and the community (*Saṅgha*) he originated (B.IV.142;V.41). Initially a novice's faith involves a willingness to take Buddhist statements concerning the Path and its goal on the basis of provisional trust. Eventually, however, everything taught must be verified or falsified in the individual's own experience. The Path of Purification is essentially a very gradual process of character development by which any person who has faith (confidence) in it can work to eliminate those impurities and defilements which result in suffering (*dukkha*) and cultivate those conditions which reveal perfection itself. Both the elimination of defilements and the cultivation of perfecting conditions, however, always entail the formation of profitable mental conditions. Faith or confidence, therefore, is a foundational condition which must accompany profitable conscious moments. Hence faith is considered a principal virtue in the list of the seven good states.

In addition to the various types of verbal, bodily and mental virtues, there are also different degrees of virtue, according to the motivations involved. For example, virtuous bodily acts undertaken out of the desire for fame are inferior to acts performed for the sake of merit. But those virtuous acts done for the sake of attaining the Noble Birth (cf. below, p. 14) or practised for the deliverance of all beings are superior virtues. On the reverse side, worthy actions can be defiled by self-praise or by disparagement of others and consequently can lead to diminution and stagnation of profitable mental formations rather than to conditions which lead to penetration of the goal of Nibbāna (B.I.33-39). So one must be mindful of the benefits one seeks in the accomplishment of virtue.

The positive fruits of virtue are abundant. Virtue purifies one's physical and verbal acts, makes one respectful, inspires confidence in what one is doing, thinking and feeling without a trace of remorsefulness, can lead to rebirth in the heavenly spheres of this *saṃsāric* universe, and finds support among good friends who are always supportive of the Path. Buddhaghosa summarizes the benefits virtue brings through the imagery of cleansing water. No river, he writes, can wash out the stain of the impure, be it the Ganges or the Yamuna; only virtue's water can cleanse and soothe man's fever in this world (B.I.24). But the most important fruit of virtue is that it composes (B.I.20) the mind and its constituents in such a way that focused concentration (*samādhi*) and insight meditation (*paññā*) become possible.

CONCENTRATION (*SAMĀDHI*)

Concentration (*samādhi*), the second major component of the Path of Liberation, refers to those kinds of contemplative acts which bring together in a unified and undistracted focus all pure mental formations. Concentration meditation is a distinctive mental act which centres the consciousness and its attendant conditions on a single object in order to effect a balanced and calm unification of profitable mental formations (B.III.2ff.).[2] The chief characteristic of a concentrated mental act is unwavering non-distraction, a pacification of all mental turbulence. The chief value for the meditator lies in the concentrated focus it effects in consciousness, a focus which enables him eventually to attentively penetrate the Truth (Nibbāna). Although the specific meditative techniques we are about to discuss can be by-passed by some followers of the Path—it is possible to follow a direct course from virtue to insight wisdom (*vipassanā paññā*)—nonetheless, some form of a profitable unification of the mind must be achieved if one is to attain penetration of the Truth. The following techniques are means to that end.

Some techniques of concentration-meditation work primarily to eliminate distraction and impediments that preclude a focused mind. Other techniques usually involve a process of withdrawal from sensory input and are intended to directly induce states of trance (*jhāna*). Among the latter type, Buddhaghosa describes ten devices (*kasina*) that can be used as the basis or support for meditation (B.IV.1ff.): earth, water, fire, air, blue, yellow, red, white, light and space. The earth device, for example, consists of a circle of earth, such as clay, of even colour and texture, shaped into the form and size of a saucer-like circle. The water device might be a bowl or water pot filled to the brim with clear water; the blue device a piece of blue cloth; the light and space device a hole in a wall.

The meditator first selects a quiet and secluded place, sits cross-legged, reminds himself of the virtue of meditation, and then proceeds to gaze attentively at the selected device. After gazing at the device for a considerable time he begins to memorize its form until he clearly sees the object in all its detail even with his eyes shut. This eidetic image is what is concentrated upon in beginning meditation. While constantly seeking to overcome various hindrances to his meditation, such as sleep, distraction, or desiring images of other objects, the meditator gradually becomes more adept and the memorized image becomes transformed into a representational (or counterpart) sign. This image is a more abstract representation of the original device. The earth device appears as a shining disk; the water device as a mirror in the sky. As abstract representations these images can be expanded or contracted in size by the imaging mind. The meditator who can do this now has access to the first state of trance. As his meditation continues to stabilize, he becomes absorbed in this first trance (B.IV.32ff.).

In this trance, the previously mentioned hindrances are eliminated. The meditator is completely concentrated upon the representational sign-object. He experiences pleasures and enthusiasm and is able to engage in lucid discursive reasoning including thoughts about his own present condition. Continuing his meditative progression, he eventually enters the second trance. Here the meditator suppresses what he then recognizes as the distraction of reasoning and no longer thinks *about* the trance state. Rather, he becomes totally involved in it. In the third trance he eliminates the distraction of his own enthusiasm and finally reaches the fourth trance state when he transcends even his sense of pleasure, thereby abiding in pure and absolute concentration. Now all mental formations are evenly and rightly focused on the representational sign-object. A one-pointedness of consciousness has been achieved.

A meditator may then carry his absorption beyond this fourth trance state into what is called the four formless realms (B.X.1ff.). To do this he must rid himself of the representational sign upon which he is focusing. Consequently, he expands the sign-object image in all directions, and then turns his attention to the boundless space touching the limits of the sign-object. Concentrating on the boundless space he enters the fifth trance state. Beyond this, he may then concentrate on unlimited consciousness (sixth), then nothingness (seventh), and finally reach the eighth state of neither-perception-nor-non-perception, with peace and calm being the dominant concomitant of consciousness. At this stage the mental formations have reached a state of extreme subtlety, characterized by equanimity and unified focus. A ninth trance, called the 'cessation of perception and feeling' (*nirodha samāpatti*), is a state in which the meditator becomes totally without thought or feeling. This trance state essentially develops the meditator's ability to sustain and enjoy the benefits of Nibbānic awareness once attainment has been experienced. I shall refer to this again later.

Different in kind from these device techniques (earth, water, and so on) leading to trance are the techniques of concentration meditation that function primarily to eliminate distraction and impediments that prevent the development of virtue and balanced mental formations.[3] Like the device technique, however, these methods are selected on the basis of the individual's temperament. To counteract the defilement of greed, for example, a meditation on ugliness (that is, the ten stages of the decomposition of a corpse) may be recommended by a meditation master or by a good friend. A meditation subject suitable to someone of a hateful temperament is that of loving-kindness. This meditation subject, in fact, is suitable for everyone (B.III.57ff.) and is the first of four closely associated contemplations: love (*mettā*), compassion (*karuṇā*), sympathetic joy (*muditā*) and equanimity (*upekkhā*) (B.IX.1ff.). These are sometimes called the abodes of Brahmā as their attainment leads to rebirth in the Brahmā heavens.

The procedure of the love-meditation is, briefly, as follows. The meditator begins by consciously reviewing the dangers of hate and the advantages of patience. Then he directs the attitude of loving-kindness toward himself, thinking: 'May I be happy and kind.' It is important at this early stage for one not to attempt to extend the meditation of love toward one's spouse or an enemy, because the former may turn into desire and the latter into hate. The meditator must first fortify himself with love and kindness. Following that, he can expand the range of his love toward those in his house, to the people in the village, and gradually extend his loving thoughts to the whole world, embracing all beings (B.III.58).

If, during the course of his love meditation, hateful thoughts arise in his mind, the meditator should contemplate the Buddha's teachings on loving-kindness. Eventually the meditator reaches a stage where he expands his love to the whole world equally. At this stage he approaches the first trance (*jhāna*) and soon becomes absorbed in it.[4] While in this first trance the meditator is intent upon the entire world with a consciousness imbued with loving-kindness, free from enmity and affliction. The advantages of this absorption state are interesting and varied. One who gains it sleeps in comfort, wakes in comfort, dreams no bad dreams, is dear to human and non-human beings; deities guard him, fire, poison and weapons do not affect him, his mind is easily concentrated, the expression on his face is serene, he dies unconfused, and if he penetrates no higher he will be reborn in the Brahmā world (B.IX.60ff.).

Other calming meditations Buddhaghosa discusses are mindfulness of breathing and of death, remembrance of peace and the three jewels (the Buddha, *Dhamma, Saṅgha*), and many others, all of which are processes for calming the mind and focusing the mental formations in profitable ways. Practice of such techniques in concentration-meditation, by bringing unification and undistracted balance to consciousness and its concomitants, enables one to easily advance toward insight wisdom, the third major component of the Path of Liberation.

INSIGHT WISDOM (*VIPASSANĀ PAÑÑĀ*

Virtue is the beginning, concentration the middle, and wisdom the end of all profitable things (B.I.10ff.). Wisdom (*paññā*) is developed through the practice of insight-meditation which complements but differs from concentration-meditation. The latter, as we have seen, cultivates successive stages of trance meant to calm the mind and purify it from defilements. Insight-meditation, however, is not transic *withdrawal* from manifold sense experiences, but a process of analytical *observation* and insight (*vipassanā*) into the sensory world and beyond.[5] Insight-meditation, in sum, is an analytical method of mindful observation into the nature of all phenomena. Its final purpose is to enable the mind to penetrate (*paṭivedha*) through to the true nature of all that is, thus leading to the discovery of the Truth of Nibbāna.

With the focused and balanced mental ability the meditator has developed up to this point, an objective and dispassionate analysis of the individual character of all mental and material states can be undertaken. The nature of mentality, those immaterial states of consciousness and accompanying conditions, are observed and can be analyzed in the following way. The insight-meditator examines all the sense doors through which the mind observes and reacts to phenomena. He perceives that visible data, for example, give rise to a visual consciousness—eye-consciousness, which is but one type of consciousness and is activated by the eye sense-organ. Upon further analysis, the meditator comes to understand that eye-consciousness may constitute but one single thought moment which is followed in rapid succession by other moments of consciousness, visual or otherwise. The mind itself [6] is seen, through the direct perception of the meditator, to be essentially nothing but a rapid succession of individual units of types of consciousness: that is, a cognitive series (*citta-vīthi*) of thought moments.

Reflection upon this series of directly perceived thought moments results in the following type of descriptive analysis of an act of seeing:[7]

/B/C/U/P/V/S/T/N/J/J/J/J/J/J/J/L/L/

'B' indicates *bhavaṅga*, the mind in its sleeping state: that is, a posited moment of subliminal consciousness before the arising of attentive, cognitive moments. 'C' is *calana*, the vibration of that sleeping state; 'U' is *upaccheda*, the interruptive, awakening moment; 'P' is *pañcadvārāvajjana*, the thought-moment that inquires from which of the five sense doors the particular object is coming to mind; 'V' is *viññāṇa*, consciousness (here, eye-consciousness), the moment of bare cognition separated from feelings, perceptions and other mental concomitants for the sake of analysis; 'S', *sampaṭicchana*, the assimilation of the object (in this instance, visible datum) by consciousness; 'T', *saṃtīraṇa*, determining what the object is; 'N', *votthapana*, concluding what the object is.

The next seven moments are *javanas* ('J'). They are the active moments of the thought process, the moments of alert intellection. It is at this active stage of the cognitive series that *kamma* is actualized. Depending upon the type of conscious response to the given visible datum, good or bad *kamma* occurs (for example, seeing a good friend or seeing an enemy). Following the production of *kamma*, 'L' or *tadālambanas* is a mental registration of this cognitive experience. Thereafter the mind returns to its initial subliminal state.

The speed of this process of thoughts is almost instantaneous and only a meditator with a highly skilled and focused mind can directly penetrate to this insight. According to Buddhaghosa,[8] the time duration involved in the rise and fall of one physical moment is equivalent to sixteen conscious moments. Hence, when one performs a conscious physical act, good or bad, thousands of thought moments occur, each with its own accompanying conditions. If these attendant conditions are composed of volition, concentration, faith and mindfulness, the active 'J' moments of the cognitive series will result in a great number of good *kammas*. Such may occur when seeing a good friend. However, suppose one sees his enemy. The constituents of the mental formation of each thought moment may involve, unless one is advanced on the Path, volition accompanied by hate (*dosa*) or other agitating conditions. The result is a series of bad *kammas*.

By means of this type of penetrating analysis of mentality, the Buddhist who is practising insight-meditation realizes that in the mental sphere there is nothing over and above the processes of thought formations. There is no thinker behind the thoughts; there is only a complex series of thought moments. The meditator *sees* that there is no substantial essence underlying individual mental phenomena, and after exploring the nature of material events as well, attains to the insight that mentality and materiality are essentially matrices of interdependent, momentary and conditioned events (called *dhammas*) which are impermanent, without substantial essence, and therefore not to be craved after or attached to.

Further development of insight-meditation continues this method of penetrating observation and direct comprehension of the phenomenal world. Insight wisdom arises, and the meditator *sees* the causal interrelatedness of all phenomena (*paticca samuppāda*) and that all of existence is characterized by impermanence (*anicca*), suffering (*dukkha*) and non-self (*anatta*). He understands that the view of the 'annihilationist' (one who only sees the passing away of conditions) does not account for the observed continuity of momentary events, but that the view of the 'eternalist' (one who does not see the passing away of conditions) does not properly account for the rise and fall of momentary occurrences (B.XIII.74). Therefore he directs his efforts along the Middle Path, and continues to internalize through direct insight such teachings as: suffering is not the self; all conditioned things are empty and full of danger when their true nature is not perceived; safety and happiness lie in detachment from things; there is no 'I' or 'me' anywhere; and no 'thing' is to be taken as an object of thought (B.XVIII–XXII).

The insight meditator, by means of the wisdom he has begun to establish and based on the purifications realized through the practices of virtue and concentration, is now able to change the character of the mental formations that occur in his thought processes. Knowing that all phenomena are an interrelated flux of dependent conditions void of any unique, permanent identity, the meditator is able to call this attention at the outset of his own process of thought moments when sense data arouse the mind. Comparing it to our previous example of seeing something, the cognitive series modified by insight wisdom would be as follows:

/B/C/U/M/J/J/J/J$_g$/J$_m$/J$_p$/J$_p$/B/B/B/B/B/B/

'B', 'C', and 'U' indicate the *bhavaṅga* moments when the subliminal consciousness is aroused and awakened. 'M' designates the moment of 'mind-door attention' (*mano-dvārāvajjana*) and supplants the former *pañcadvārāvajjana* ('P') thought-moment that inquired into the five sense doors which eventually led to the determination of what was the sense-datum object coming to mind. Rather than seeking an object, which gives rise to eye-consciousness (*viññāṇa, 'V'*), the insightful mind is attentive at this moment and sees the sense datum for what it truly is, namely: impermanent, suffering and non-self. Such an analytical thought moment is accompanied by the conditions of equanimity and neutrality toward the sense datum now properly understood (B.XXI.129). In Buddhaghosa's words, the 'thick murk that hides the truths has been dispelled' and the meditator's 'consciousness no longer enters into or settles down on or resolves upon any field of formations at all, nor clings, cleaves or clutches on to it . . .' (B.XXII.4).

The *javanas* ('J's), the active moments of cognition, immediately follow this moment of mindful attention ('M'), displacing those thought moments that dealt with the datum as object in the previously mentioned series (cf. 'S', 'T' and 'N'). The first three *javanas* are composed of the same mental constituents that the mind-attentive thought-moment is, namely, the conditions of resolute faith (*saddhā*), increased stability in mindfulness and concentration, and energetic, refined wisdom. The remaining *javanas* in this cognitive series go beyond the realm of *saṃsāra,* beyond the lineage of the ordinary man and belong to 'seeing' or realizing Nibbāna.

The first of these remaining *javana* moments is accompanied by the 'change of lineage' condition ('g', *gotrabhū*); the second by 'knowledge of the Path' ('m', *magga nāna*). The last two active moments of comprehension enjoy, ever so briefly, this fruition attainment of the Path ('p', *phala*). The meditator's ability to sustain as well as attain the benefit of this momentary disclosure of *Nibbāna* is dependent upon all previous practices in virtue, concentration and wisdom. But it was specifically the ninth trance state of 'cessation of all thoughts and feelings' that was preparatory for sustaining the impact of these 'trans-*saṃsāric*' moments (B.XXIII.16ff.). Following this brief fruition, the mind process returns to *bhavaṅga*.

This is the meditator's first time to realize *Nibbāna*. Now he is a Stream-entrant and has reached the first of the four Noble Paths (Stream-entrant, Once-returner, No-returner and Arahant) (B.XXII.1ff). He has experienced the Noble Birth (*ariyāya jātiyā jāto*) and is a son of the Buddha (*Buddhassa orasa putta bhāvaṃ āvahati*).

He has cut off all defilements completely, piercing and exploding the mass of greed (*lobha*), hate (*dosa*) and delusion (*moha*) that prevents Nibbāna from emerging. In these thought moments he has left the stream of *saṃsāra* and has entered the stream of Nibbāna.

Continuing his meditation he further deepens and stabilizes his insights, eventually attaining to the second, third and fourth Noble Paths. As a Once-returner he is totally free from all self-centred consciousness, doubts and wrong views; as a No-returner he completely rids himself of craving even for desirable states of accomplishment; as an Arahant he becomes perfect in all good qualities. At this culminating stage, the meditator-Arahant sees and fully understands the meaning and nature of suffering (*dukkha*), the causes for its arising and cessation, and the Path of Purification and Liberation that leads to its cessation: that is, the Four Noble Truths taught by Gautama the Buddha.[9] The Arahant's virtue (*sīla*), concentration (*samādhi*) and wisdom (*paññā*) are pure and complete; he has discovered that which is even beyond all attainments, Nibbāna, the end and goal of the Buddhist Path of Liberation from suffering.

Notes

1. Buddhaghosa reflects the scholastic *Abhidhamma* aspect of the early Buddhist tradition. Cf. Bhadantācariya Buddhaghosa, *The Path of Purification* (*Visuddhimagga*), trans. Bhikkhu Nyāṇamoli, Vols. I & II (Berkeley & London, 1976), henceforth cited as 'B', followed by chapter and paragraph numbers. For the Pāli edition of the text, see *Visuddhimagga*, Vols. I & II, ed. Mrs Rhys Davids in the Pāli Text Society Series (London, 1920-21, reprint).

This present study is most deeply indebted to the scholarship of Dr Shanta Ratnayaka. His manuscript *Two Ways of Perfection: Buddhist and Christian*, which is being published in Colombo, Sri Lanka, constitutes a major source of information and clarification regarding Buddhaghosa's exposition of the Buddhist path.

2. Cf. Ratnayaka, *Two Ways of Perfection*, pp. 55ff.

3. Buddhaghosa co-ordinates the two types of meditation subjects, however. For someone of a hateful temperament, for example, the four colour devices and the four contemplations beginning with loving-kindness (cf. text below) are prescribed (B.III.121).

4. Note should be made of the view of some Western scholars that meditations on the four contemplations cannot lead into trance states because they are different in kind. Cf., e.g., Stephan V. Beyer's well-conceived outline of Buddhaghosa's exposition in his essay 'The Doctrine of Meditation in the

Hīnayāna' in *Buddhism: A Modern Perspective,* ed. Charles S. Prebish (Pennsylvania, 1975), pp. 137-47.

5. Cf. Beyer, op. cit., p. 137.

6. Buddhaghosa uses the terms for mind, consciousness, cognizing, interchangeably. He explicitly states: 'The words *viññāṇa*(consciousness), *citta* (mind), and *mano* (mind) are one in meaning'. Cf. B.XIV.82. For further clarification, see B.XIV.82,n.35.

7. Cf., e.g., B.I.57ff.; IV.33ff. and n.13; IV.74ff. as well as the citations in the text. This particular expository format follows very closely S. Ratnayaka's analysis. Cf. above, fn.1.

8. Cf. Buddhaghosa's commentary on the *Vibhaṅga,* pp. 25-26. Cited by David J. Kalupahana in his *Buddhist Philosophy: A Historical Analysis* (Honolulu, 1976), p. 102.

9. The eight factors of the Noble Eightfold Path as enumerated in the doctrine of the Four Noble Truths are simply a different schema for the three essentials of Buddhist training and discipline I have discussed. Morality (*sīla*) incorporates right speech, right action and right livelihood; concentration (*samādhi*) includes right effort, right mindfulness (or attentiveness) and right concentration; wisdom (*paññā*) consists of right thought and right understanding.

Heinrich Dumoulin

Buddhism—A Religion of Liberation

BUDDHISM is a religion of liberation. It is concerned with liberating man from his state of suffering. From this basic point of view it is similar to Christianity which is also concerned with man's plight and seeks his liberation. Yet, right from the start one notices an essential difference between the two religions. For a Buddhist, the universal state of misery means man's sorry existence in this world of constant becoming (*saṃsāra*), while for a Christian this state is the result of 'original sin'; that is, man's freely committed sin at the origin of human history. This is why Christianity, from the very beginning, brings into play the historical category which is of its essence, whereas Buddhism stresses the existential aspect of the human condition. This diversity not only affects the concept of the universal state of misery but just as much the concept of liberation in the two world-religions. Christianity provides a history of salvation, while in Buddhism the dominant part is played by the religious experiences of existence.

KARMA AT THE ROOT OF MAN'S WRETCHEDNESS

The founder of Buddhism expressed his experience of the total wretchedness of human existence and the path that leads to liberation in the four noble truths of his Benares sermon. The first truth states that human wretchedness is all-embracing and inexorable. The second truth, however, reveals the cause of this suffering: 'It is the thirst for pleasure, for becoming, for non-existence which, accompanied by sensual joy and occasionally finding satisfaction, causes rebirth in the way of becoming'. This is logically followed by the third truth which is the elimination of the cause of suffering, while the fourth truth deals with the cessation of suffering and thus with the path towards liberation. The wording of the second noble truth shows that in original Buddhism the basic experience of suffering was already linked in the earliest tradition with the ancient Indian pre-Buddhist idea of reincarnation in the cycle of existences, and this idea is then again inextricably linked with the idea of *karma*. In both cases we have here popular Vedic notions which cannot be considered as typically Buddhist truths, either in their origin or in their essence. Yet, whenever early Buddhist writings entail the truth of suffering they always have recourse to these ideas of *karma* and reincarnation. Human existence is full of suffering primarily because it is spurred on by thirst and desire. This desire has power over man as long as he is dominated by the law of *karma* and is reborn in the cycle of existences.

The Sanskrit term *karma* originally meant 'deed', 'doing', and at an early date involved cause-and-effect in the action: every action has an effect, and every effect is caused by some action. In ancient India, e.g., in the Upanishads, the *karma* concept already had a religio-ethical connotation: a good action produces a good fruit, evil action, however, produces evil and suffering. Retribution, implied in *karma,* reaches beyond the present life on earth and spans the three phases of time: past, present and future.

In Buddhism the *karma* concept is linked with the doctrine of the twelve phases of the chain which binds man's coming into being in a state of dependency (*pratītya samutpāda*). Two links of this chain, namely ignorance and thirst, drive the cyclic course through the three phases of time (as above) and the six realms of being (heavenly bodies, human beings, demons, hungry spirits, animals, hell). Reincarnation in any of these realms corresponds to the *karma,* the way life has been led. Buddhist teaching distinguishes a 'good *karma*' and an 'evil *karma*'. To the good *karma* or good behaviour corresponds a 'pleasant effect', but the good *karma* remains within the sphere of suffering existence in the world of becoming, although it helps to make progress towards liberation. This world of becoming, dominated by the law of *karma,* is a state of wretchedness according to the Buddhist way of thinking. With the psychological subtlety characteristic of old Indian wisdom, Buddhist teaching made a distinction with regard to the kinds of *karma*, which brings it closer to Christian ideas. Of the three kinds of *karma*, namely the *karma* of the body, of the mouth and of the will, the first two which, through the body and the mouth, reveal intent, are called 'revealing *karma*'. This is distinguished from 'non-revealing *karma*', which is described as an inclination which remains behind after the deed, in the way of a habit. This inclination is associated with man's passions and can easily lead to wrong doing. This reminds one of the Christian doctrine of concupiscence which leaves traces after a sin has been committed and invites to further sin.

DIFFICULTIES AND NEW INTERPRETATIONS OF THE KARMA CONCEPT

The *karma* concept, like the idea of original sin, is difficult to grasp in its complexity. Buddhist interpretations branched out in several directions and so allowed for numerous interpretations. Just as Christian theology seeks a new understanding of the teaching about original sin in order to meet a changing modern mentality, so modern Buddhism is looking for a view of *karma* to which modern man can respond. Both the doctrine of original sin and the notion of *karma* contain a mythical element in their traditional interpretation. For centuries the doctrine of original sin was based on the legendary narrative in Genesis of the state of man in paradise and the fall of our first parents. Modern exegesis, supported by the natural sciences, recognized the myth as an etiological explanation of man's dire state, as the scriptural authors found it. The difficulty created by accepting sin as a matter of procreation, although sin is always a matter of free human decision, was avoided by the monogenetic interpretation of the original of the human race.

1. In the wake of the modern ways of thinking, brought about partly by scientific knowledge and partly through our changing attitude towards life in a technological age, and affecting all world religions, the ideas of *karma* and reincarnation were pushed into the background. Without any doubt, both these ideas are strongly conditioned by the mythical element. Recent Buddhist scholars therefore hold that modern *demythologization* is imperative. And here they show themselves no less radical than their Western contemporaries. They do not abandon the thought of just retribution, but have a very critical approach towards those instances of retribution which are related in their scriptural tradition. Today's Buddhist writing shows only rare references to the six realms of existence which were so popular in earlier times.

2. The ideas of *karma* and reincarnation are linked with a *cyclical concept of history* which can be understood in a nihilistic sense, as Nietzsche did in his myth of the 'eternal return of the same'. But, as understood in the Far East, this concept, though linked with the path towards religious salvation, is in no way nihilistic. And yet, it does not fit in with modern anthropology because this anthropology assigns priority to man's historicity. For centuries the West, inspired by the Greek thought integrated into Christianity, clung to a teleological concept of history which saw mankind as deliberately striving towards its fulfilment. In modern times the interest in the natural and historical process of evolution increased. Evolutionary theories of history became popular. Today many Buddhists show themselves critical of the doctrine of reincarnation as they recognize the importance of man's historical dimension. Phenomena which point in this direction are interpreted in psychological terms, just as, on the whole, modern

psychology shows great interest in the idea of reincarnation. It is well known that Jung found many of his discoveries confirmed in the Tibetan Book of the Dead which describes the wanderings of the dead through the Bardo regions.

3. A third difficulty arises from the moral components of the *karma* idea. It is true that the first meaning of *karma* is 'doing', 'act', but from earliest times it also contained the moral dimension of the human act. This means that from the philosophical angle it involves the problem of *freedom*. Buddhism does not deny free will but the ambiguity of the *karma* idea is abundantly reflected in Buddhist literature. If *karma* continues to operate throughout the three phases of time: that is, if past actions have a direct and determining effect on the present, there is no room for the freedom of the individual. Guilt contracted in previous existences necessarily works through succeeding generations. Modern Buddhists who understand that without a free will there can be no moral, responsible human behaviour refuse to accept the popular belief in fate which is based on the ideas of *karma* and reincarnation. In their view, the deterministic belief in fate contradicts the very meaning implied in the *karma* idea which points to the future and spurs man on to moral effort. They therefore look for a new more satisfactory interpretation of the *karma* concept.

NEW INTERPRETATIONS IN THE LIGHT OF BUDDHIST-CHRISTIAN DIALOGUE

The new interpretations of the Buddhist *karma* concept, like the attempts to arrive at a new understanding of the teaching on original sin, are significant for the dialogue between the two world-religions. When outlining the basic difference between the two I mentioned the categories of the historical and the existential. The new interpretations of the doctrine on original sin clearly tone down the historical. Without in any way diminishing the fact that Christianity is essentially salvation history—its ultimate answer lies in a historical factual event—many historical aspects are today toned down as the inevitable result of demythologization. Instead of the legendary Genesis narrative, the attempt to provide a modern and more satisfying explanation of the teaching on original sin concentrates on the way in which 'human existence is situated' in an environment marked by 'the sin of the world' (Piet Schoonenberg). A Buddhist, too, can experience this situational existence in so far as he considers the element of human sinfulness which is not wholly alien to his own religion. On the other hand, the attempts of modern Buddhists to bring about an understanding of the *karma* concept which is free from myth and superstition show points where they come closer to the Christian view of the world.

Ultimately the *karma* concept means the general intertwining of all human behaviour, the weaving of an unfathomable, impenetrable yet meaningful net with all its connecting lines running in every direction. This experience is in no way alien to Christianity. Ever since the Epistle to the Romans, Christian literature has often brought out the solidarity of mankind, that interrelationship which is first of all experienced in the radical wretchedness of human existence but then opens up a hopeful looking forward towards salvation. Both Buddhism and Christianity, profoundly involved in the fact of suffering, are aware of a human solidarity in suffering and a universality of salvation.

The Buddhist view does not limit this solidarity to mankind but draws the whole cosmos within the scope of the changing interrelationship. Paul, too, speaks of 'creation groaning in travail' (*Romans* 8:22). Obviously it is here only a question of the two views getting closer. But the striving after a better understanding of original sin and *karma* today brings out the universality of the condition of suffering and the consequent solidarity among men of all times and all climes as part of the universal human experience in both Christianity and Buddhism.

Buddhist-Christian dialogue throws new light on the widely-differing outlook, concepts and emotional reactions of East and West. It can easily end up in a blind alley when the partners of the dialogue cling to certain notions. In his inner experience a religious man realizes the depth of the mystery of suffering. Buddhist scriptures assure man repeatedly that human understanding cannot penetrate the comprehensive entanglement of *karma*. According to the Pali canon, the knowledge of all the *karma* relationships is one of the three wondrous kinds of knowledge which Buddha attained with his enlightenment. In his second Epistle to the Thessalonians (2:7) Paul writes about the 'mystery of iniquity' (*mysterium iniquitatis*). For the Christian this mystery is illuminated when he considers the 'mystery of the cross' which according to Paul is, to the human mind, folly and a scandal (cf. I Cor.1:18ff.). Here the dialogue gets into an unfathomable depth.

THE WAY TOWARDS LIBERATION

The basic difference between Christianity and Buddhism, namely, the historical orientation of the one and the existential outlook of the other, also marks their view of liberation and redemption respectively. If we limit ourselves to the early Buddhist view, we find the way towards liberation set out principally in the fourth of the four noble truths in the Benares sermon: 'This, you, monks, is the noble truth of the way towards the cessation of suffering. It is this noble eightfold path, which is said to be: right belief, right purpose, right speech, right behaviour, right calling (or occupation), right endeavour, right contemplation, right concentration'.

The teaching of the eightfold path needs no complicated interpretation. Simply understood the first six points cover the morally good human life in word, deed and disposition, a triplet which became very popular in later Buddhism. Man takes this path on his own decision and with a sincere purpose. Moral behaviour lies within the scope of his own ability. The seventh point, right contemplation, represents a transition to the experience of meditation, which is achieved with the eighth point, right concentration. According to the early Buddhists, meditation also lies within man's scope.

The positive aspect of the progress along the eightfold path has a corresponding negative aspect which deals with the clearing of obstacles which obstruct liberation in man's existence. Buddha spoke of obstacles which the disciple has to get rid of at all cost. The same text which contains the exposition of the eightfold path speaks of thirst or desire, which is the cause of all suffering and therefore of the wretched existence of man. Later on the teaching of this aspect was elaborated and the eliminating process implied in liberation was spelt out in detail in a complicated system. The decision to follow the path towards liberation meant commitment to the process of redemption, a process of detachment and denial, which implied the moral disposition but worked towards higher stages, even the ultimate. The most intense effort was required in meditation, which contains the ultimate liberation from even the most subtle obstacles which spring from man's congenital egocentrism.

According to early Buddhist sources, man proceeds on the way towards liberation alone, without any outside help, simply on the strength of his own effort. This turns the Buddhist path to salvation into self-redemption, and, in fact, the redeeming of the self through the self.

Modern philosophers have taken this as the realization of their vision of man as autonomous. Yet two things should not be ignored. First of all, there is a distinction between theoretical doctrine and religious practice, which can be observed everywhere in Buddhism. One cannot exclude the fact that, when a large number of faithful practise a theoretical doctrine of self-redemption, in actual practice an 'other force', namely transcendence, asserts itself. Some early Buddhist art, e.g., some sculptures of Bhārhut and Sānchī (second century BC), point this way.

It is equally important to see that the final stage of the way towards liberation was already open to this transcendency in very early Buddhism and, I feel I may say, in Buddha's own mind.

THE ULTIMATE STATE OF LIBERATION

No other Buddhist word has been so early and so generally taken up in the West as *nirvana*. It is the word for the final state of man in Buddhism. This may well be the only thing we can say about it with any certainty. Neither Buddhists nor non-Buddhists have ever agreed on the essence of *nirvana* in spite of much research and tedious long-drawn-out controversies. Etymologically, *nirvana* is a negative word. The verb *va*, meaning 'blow' (as the wind blows), is attached to the negative prefix *nir* and is applied in Buddhist literature to fire which is doused, to stars that set, and to the sacred or holy which 'goes beyond'. Yet, Buddhist and non-Buddhist scholars agree that neither the etymology of the word nor the analogies with which it is illustrated convey the full meaning of *nirvana*.

The popular view is that *nirvana* simply means an end to suffering and the cessation of earthly suffering when the final stage is reached. Buddhist faithful see it as a happy condition of profound rest and imperturbable peace. The West often sees *nirvana* as 'extinction'. This version not only means the cessation of suffering but the extinction of the fire of lust, and therefore of the cause of suffering. But, according to many students of Buddhism, it goes beyond this and implies extinction in general: that is, the extinction of awareness, of individuality and of existence. Eventually this nihilistic interpretation of *nirvana* spread widely throughout the West but also occurs in some philosophical schools of Hīnayāna Buddhism. It is remarkable that none of the first modern European Buddhologists (H. T. Colebrooke, B. H. Hodgson, A. Csoma Körös, E. Burnouf) saw the final state of *nirvana* as total annihilation, although they were aware of the difficulties inherent in Buddhist terminology.

Many early Buddhist texts seem close to accepting, not the total extinction of existence, but a radical change in the way of existing as the meaning of *nirvana*. In the context of ideas about reincarnation and *karma*, *nirvana* means the escape from a wretched existence in *samsāra*, the escape from the cycle of reincarnations and the breaking of the bonds imposed by *karma*, all important phases which are frequently mentioned in the Buddhist canon and which open up a positive view of the final state of man in Buddhism.

One may accept that the vast majority of faithful Buddhists saw *nirvana* as a happy ending. Early Buddhist praise of *nirvana* should not be underrated as poetical decoration of the doctrine. It is far more the heartfelt response of the faithful to the message of ultimate liberation. In any case it can claim as much persuasive force as philosophical speculation which leans towards nihilism. At present research has not got beyond guesswork in regard to early or late dating within the Buddhist canon.

The modern understanding of Buddhism prefers the positive interpretation of *nirvana,* particularly in Japan, the part of Asia where the trend towards modernization has made most progress. Two aspects ought to be mentioned which make the positive nature of the final state more acceptable to the modern Buddhist. First of all, there is a connection between *nirvana* and states of meditation which are achieved through strenuous exercise and are highly esteemed in Buddhism. The fourth stage of *dhyāna* was always seen as a kind of anticipation of *nirvana.* Apart from an entry to the state of *nirvana* at the hour of death, the early Buddhists knew of a *'nirvana* here and now' which could be attained in the present life. Every school of Mahāyana Buddhism knows of and practises meditation which leads to experiences of enlightenment resembling *nirvana.* When one looks at the whole development of Buddhism in its many schools the term 'liberation' seems an acceptable translation of *nirvana.* This term was adopted by Vatican II in its *Declaration on the Relationship of the Church with non-Christian Religions,* at the wish of the Japanese bishops. The word obviously cannot express the ineffable nature of the state of *nirvana* but it reflects its main effect—that which all Buddhists see as important. Buddhism as a way to salvation sees itself as a way to liberation.

This leads to the second positive aspect which comes out strongly in religious life today. People want to see in religion at large, not merely the promise of liberation in the hereafter, but something already operative here-and-now. If the eschatological orientation is essential to religion—and it is in both Buddhism and Christianity—a modern religious man insists that he should experience the liberating force of his religion in his present life. In Buddhism this comes out most in the Buddhist-inspired folk-religions. In Japan such a religion describes itself as the *'nirvana* sect' because it particularly reveres the *nirvana* Sutra and Buddha's entry into the rest of *nirvana.* This sect also shares the optimistic and activist orientation of the other charismatic folk religions.

We may say then that modern Buddhism does not see itself as a religion of extinction but as a way towards liberation. This fact is bound to influence the interpretation of *nirvana,* for, like all human words, this term is shaped by time, history and environment.

Select bibliography

E. Conze, *Buddhism: Its Essence and Development* (Oxford 1951).

J. Masson, *Le Bouddhisme* (Museum Lessianum, 1975).

H. Nakamura, 'Die Grundlehren des Buddhismus. Ihre Wurzeln in Geschichte und Tradition', in H. Dumoulin (ed.), *Buddhismus der Gegenwart* (Freiburg, 1970) ('The Basic Teachings of Buddhism', in *Buddhism in the Modern World*, H. Dumoulin, ed., New York, 1976).

H. Oldenberg, *Buddha. Sein Leben, seine Lehre, seine Gemeinde* (13th ed., Munich, 1961).

W. Rahula, *L'enseignement du Bouddha* (Paris, 1960).

C. Humphreys, *Karma and Rebirth* (London, n.d.).

W. L. King, *Buddhism and Christianity* (London, 1963).

L. de la Vallée Poussin, *Nirvana* (Paris, 1925).

G. R. Welbon, *The Buddhist Nirvana and Its Western Interpreters* (Chicago, 1968).

Frits Vos

The Discovery of the Special Nature of Buddha: Sudden Enlightenment in Zen

IN THE SPRING of 1686 Matsuo Bashō (1644–94) composed the following *haiku:*

furuike ya	An old pond—
kawazu tobikomu	a frog plunges into it:
mizu no oto	the sound of the water . . .

Several commentaries on this poem of seventeen syllables see here an analogy with the attainment of *satori* or sudden Enlightenment: eternal silence is broken by an unexpected sound, ripples appear on the water, but after a few moments the old peace has returned. The best interpretation, however, is this: the first line expresses the timeless, the second the momentary, the third is the intersection of the eternal and the temporal.[1] This intersection is the moment of the *unio mystica:*

Many poems of this kind can no doubt be compared with *zenki:* that is, means used by the masters to instruct their disciples. In essence the *haiku* can have the same function as a blow with fist or stick on the head or shoulder of the disciple or the terrifying cry of *katsu.* People often speak of Zen Buddhism: a description which implies that we are dealing here with a development of the Buddhism which originated in India, in a typically eastern Asiatic form. But this is not correct. In origin, Zen is a Chinese reaction to the Buddhist teaching of salvation, particularly influenced by Taoism. The Buddhism with which we are principally concerned in China, Korea and Japan is that of the 'Great Vehicle', or Mahāyāna. Here the world of the unreal, that is, *not* non-existent but relatively existent phenomena, and *nirvana*, 'extinction', are seen as different manifestations of the absolute becoming which lies at the root of all. This Absolute is the eternal and universal Buddha nature, with which one can identify by means of the transcendental concept of *prajñā*. Some Mahāyāna writings maintain that all living beings equally contain germs of the Buddha state and are therefore able to attain this Buddha state. Illusion, however, prevents these germs from becoming active. When illusion is destroyed the germs are activated and perfect Enlightenment will be achieved.

Various Mahāyāna sects have elaborated this basic theme in different ways. In the mystic Shingon sect, for instance, the womb world of phenomena—so called because all phenomena spring from it as from a womb—and the diamond world, that is, the world of the ideas, the higher Absolute World, are contrasted with each other. For him who reaches the highest insight there is no difference between the two worlds. This highest insight is equivalent to awakening or enlightenment.

TAOISM

The term Taoism is derived from the Chinese word *tao*, which really means 'way', but the meaning has been broadened in various senses. In China it very early came to mean 'the course of things in nature', and human behaviour was held to be closely connected with it. This therefore started from a fundamental unity of man and world—a way of looking at things which is understandable in an agricultural population. This experience of reality led to the idea that the function of a ruler was not so much a matter of governing as of maintaining a good natural order in the world. If everything, including every individual, had its right place in this natural order, then the whole would run on its own. Taoism, which certainly incorporates many of the most ancient Chinese religious notions and images, was obviously again centred on *tao*, the way or course of what occurs in nature. All that happens in nature, happens of its own, without being consciously willed or laboured for: water flows, smoke rises, and so on. Man, then, should identify with the *tao:* that is, should lose his 'self' in the process of nature. The idea of *tao* also acquires a metaphysical implication which largely corresponds to what some Western thinkers see as the Absolute. The Taoist ideal is *wu-wei*, 'to do nothing': that is, *not* not doing anything at all, but not interfering in the natural course of events. Man's intelligence, which introduces arbitrary distinctions and value-judgments, is evil because the essence of the cosmic reality cannot be grasped rationally. At the most it can be described by means of parable and paradox—as mystics have done, always and everywhere. Both original Buddhism and Taoism can be described as a teaching of personal salvation and redemption. There is, however, an important difference between the two: the follower of Taoism abandons himself in ecstasy to the great transformation, the eternal change of all things. Buddhism, on the other hand, sees true salvation in being liberated from this endless changing, and therefore in what is eternal, unchanging and one. Buddhist salvation lies in liberation from the world of appearances (phenomena), from an existence which is inseparably linked with instability and suffering, with originating and perishing, with birth and re-birth. In spite of this, Buddhism and Taoism have mutually influenced each other and the more popular Buddhist ideas and images have left clear traces in popular Taoist belief, sometimes called 'vulgar' Taoism.

There is also an interesting corresponding use of terminology in Taoism and Chinese-Japanese Buddhism. For instance, the concept of *tao* is also used by Buddhists in the sense of the Absolute, while the attainment of *nirvana* is sometimes called *tê-tao*, 'to achieve the way'.

On the other hand, this similar use of terms can also lead to misconceptions. 'Emptiness' and 'empty', for instance, mean something totally different in the two doctrines. The Sanskrit term *śūnyatā* is usually translated by 'emptiness'. It relates to the negation of a static phenomenal existence, which does not imply that the concept of 'existence' as such is denied. All existence and all its component elements, all properties, actions, ideas and images, depend on causality, and exist only in virtue of and in relation to each other—at the level of 'conventional truth'. Since the causal factors change all the time, there can be no static existence. At the highest level, inaccessible to the intellect with its analysis, separation and distinction, everything is identical, stripped of every distinguishing mark; in other words, it is 'empty'. The enlightened can, however, experience this fundamental oneness through the transcendental experience of emptiness. This brief explanation may show why the Buddhologist Stcherbatsky prefers to translate *śūnyatā* as 'relativity' rather than 'emptiness'.[2] But what does Taoism mean by 'emptiness'? In chapter XI of the *Tao-tê* we read: 'Although one can put thirty spokes into one hub, the cart is only usable because of what is not there. One can mould clay into a vessel, but the vessel is only usable because of what is not there. One can cut out doors and windows to make a house, but the house can only be of use because of what is not there.' Duyvendak makes the following comment: 'However indispensable the spokes may be for a wheel, in the end all depends on the hollow hub. However, necessary clay may be to make a vessel, it is the emptiness inside which matters. However necessary the material for windows and doors, the main thing is in the end the opening. What "is not" is therefore more important than "what is" '. The passage shows that it is wrong only to attach value to 'what is'.[3] When the Taoist is 'empty', i.e., purified of his passions and desires, he is totally filled with *tao*.[4] Here we meet with the *unio mystica* of Taoism, and this demands a whole life's endeavour. After the adept has achieved the presence of *tao* in himself, he finds that he is not different from *tao*, but one with it, and that he himself is *tao*.[5] For a Taoist, emptying (*kenosis*) is an end in itself, whereas for a Buddhist insight into the relativity of existence as phenomenal is essential.

Now that some basic features of Buddhism and Taoism have been set out and some points where they meet and others where they differ have been explained, I turn to Zen.

SATORI

The essence of Zen is to attain enlightenment through one's own effort. The way to be followed is laid down in four rules:

1. do not cling to canonical writings;
2. follow a particular tradition outside traditional teaching;
3. point straight to the human heart (spirit, the inner man);
4. attain the Buddha state through insight into your own nature.

Although Zen therefore claims to reject scriptural learning and to strive after Enlightenment outside holy writings in view of, and on the basis of, the particular tradition, one finds that the masters of Zen are always very well-read in, and have a profound knowledge of, the Buddhist *sūtras* and *śāstras,* and that there are numerous Zen writings.

I find that Zen has particular connections with the doctrine of Avataṃsaka which did not exist in India as a 'school' but sprang up in China about AD 600 and from there was introduced into Korea and Japan. According to this teaching, the Buddha-nature is latently present in all living and inanimate beings, regardless of their spiritual development. Every object in the universe is not only itself but includes every other object and is actually identical with it. Every phenomenon is related to all other phenomena, every experience includes all other experiences in a mutually interdependent and complementary relationship. All these living and inanimate beings are manifested through the 'formation of ideas', and so spring from one common source; they therefore have no firmly-defined nature of their own, and self-lessness is the highest truth.

In this teaching the highest stage but one of the development of thought is that where the distinction between the subjective formation of ideas and the objective reality is lifted: the merging of subject and object, the state beyond any specific description, without feeling and without thought. So we have here to do with a development from empirical knowledge to transcendental knowledge through which relative existence passes into absolute existence.

In a poem by the Korean priest In'o (c. 1600) we read:

> Heaven and earth are like one finger,
> All creatures are like one horse.
> When one knows this truth,
> All living creatures enjoy the same spring
> And brothers are found all over the world.

The first two lines of this poem contain the same kind of identifications found in the Avatamsaka doctrine: one drop of water has the taste of a hundred rivers; one moment embraces innumerable ages of the world (*kalpas*), and so eternity is identical with one single moment. In chapter five of the *Avatamsaka-sutra* it is said: 'Every particle contains innumerable Buddhas' and 'One can perceive a complete Buddha at the tip of a single hair'.[6]

The other rules concerning the way of Zen, the 'direct pointing to the human heart' and the 'attainment of the Buddha state through insight into one's own nature', culminate in sudden enlightenment (*satori*). Even in this life *nirvana* can be attained through the sudden breakthrough of awareness of the Absolute, achieved in a state of spiritual emptiness, in other words: the discovery of one's own Buddha nature by breaking through conscious logical thought. This enlightenment which brings about the *unio mystica* with the Buddha nature, does not imply a withdrawal from the world. On the contrary, Zen encourages the disciple to take part in life in this world. Zen monks, for instance, do hard work, such as cutting wood and farming. But this is a matter of *participation*, to be distinguished from the kind of egocentric *involvement* which tends to cause conflicts and spiritual breakdowns. To be born as a human being is a privilege in itself. The Zen disciple does not aim at anything superhuman. He does not want to become a hermit or a saint. He only wants to know how to become *completely* what he already is potentially—just as a tree grows, a fish swims, a bird flies and a cloud finds its shape. He wants to discover and regain his 'true self'.[7]

In Zen the meaning of *nirvana* as *liberation* is stronger than in Buddhism. In the reality of everyday one is aware of taking part in the absolute reality.

THE METHODS: ZAZEN, KŌAN, MONDŌ

In the second century of our era Nāgārjuna showed that no logical reasoning can attain to the knowledge of Absolute Truth. Not only the world of phenomena but such concepts as *nirvana*, Buddha and Bodhi, are *śūnya*, 'empty', as soon as they are made an object of thought and thus become one thing among other things. Enlightenment or awakening (*satori*) in Zen therefore means an intuitive insight into the essence of things, as opposed to understanding them intellectually and logically. To achieve awakening one tries therefore to break through all the distinctions and categories of logical thought.

When the disciple sits down in meditation (*zazen*) he concentrates on a theme chosen by himself or set by the master and this theme is irrational and at first sight even absurd in content. Such themes largely consist of traditional sayings of earlier masters of Zen and are called *kōan* (cases). When they take the shape of a short, swift dialogue they are called *mondō* (question-and-answer).

One has to see the invisible, do the impossible, swim on land and walk on water, then the Absolute Truth will come to man. The use of useless words can only prevent us from finding the truth. Taoism, too, which sees liberation in a return to one's essential nature, rejects logic. Words must always be defined by using other words. The *Tao-tê ching* therefore opens as follows: 'The way about which one can talk is not the eternal way. The terms which one can mention are not the eternal terms'. And in chapter thirty-two we read: 'The way has the simplicity of the nameless. As one begins to tamper with this there are (differentiating) names. And so the wise man will know where to stop. He who knows where to stop is not in danger'. This 'knowing where to stop' refers to *wu-wei:* not to interfere, i.e., not clash with *tao*.

The question of the relation between words and experiences is also particularly important in Zen.[8]

In 'normal' thought, thinking through the use of words, we connect the prejudices inherent in these words with our fundamental experiences. Zen aims at breaking through this way of thinking. The Zen problems, *kōan*, put into words are therefore essentially rational, although the use of the words looks irrational. Thanks to the *kōan* the disciple can achieve the same inner experience as his master. One day 'the silent lifting of a finger' will be enough for him. One of the most famous *kōan* is perhaps the following: 'Zen is like a man who hangs by his teeth from a branch over an abyss. His hands have no hold, his feet no support, and underneath the tree another man asks him: ''Why did Bodhidharma[9] come from India to China?'' If the man hanging from the branch does not answer he is at fault. If he *does* answer he will fall and lose his life. What should he do?'[10] A particularly interesting example of a *mondō* is linked with the life of the Korean Zen priest Kyŏnghō (second half of the nineteenth century). His mind was badly nettled by a well-known passage from the biography of the Chinese Zen Master Ling-yün Chih-ch'ing (ninth century) who was said to have attained enlightenment by gazing at a peach-blossom. The passage in question runs as follows: 'The Master said: ''The matter of the ass is hardly out of the way when the question of the horse is already with us'' '. The meaning of this is: what has passed before and what is now here is only the same. This statement refers to the constant practicing of the Zen disciple. Kyŏnghō locked himself up in the Zen monastery Tonghak-sa in Kongju and concentrated with all his might on this problem. From time to time he even tortured himself. After three months he overheard by chance the following conversation between another priest and his father (and here follows the real *mondō*):

Father: 'Do you know the principle that if a monk does not fulfil his duties correctly he will become an ox after his death?'
Priest: 'I haven't studied that question. But since I only live on temple gifts, I could surely become something else?'
F.: 'You couldn't answer. Do you still give that kind of reply after having been a monk for tens of years?'
P.: 'I don't know this Zen-principle. So what must I say?'
F.: 'That even if you become an ox you don't have to have your nose pierced!'

Through this conversation Kyŏnghō really understood the meaning of Zen. Well known is his saying: 'The drinking of wine and the eating of meat do not prevent *prajñā;* committing a theft and leading a dissolute sexual life do not render Enlightenment impossible.' [11] Here we find a similar amoral (*not* immoral) attitude as in Taoism. In what was said about Taoism above it was already mentioned that the introduction of value-judgments and distinctions on one's own through the intellect is evil. This holds for Zen since such a mental activity is the result of thinking in categories, and of a logical dualism. To illustrate this danger we turn again to a Korean tradition.

One of the most important, and certainly one of the most remarkable, Buddhist priests of Korea was Wŏnhyo, who lived from 617 to 686. Like many other priests of his time his ideal was to go and study in China.

When in 661 he arrived with his colleague Ūisang at a port southwest of present-day Seoul, where they were to wait for a ship bound for China, night had already fallen. In the darkness they looked for shelter and found an empty house where they went to sleep. In the middle of the night Wŏnhyo woke up with a burning thirst. Groping around in the room he fortunately found a bowl with wonderfully fresh water. At daybreak it appeared that both priests had spent the night in a tomb and that the bowl was a human skull. Nauseated, Wŏnhyo vomited but at the same moment had the following insight: 'When consciousness (the heart) arises, the various phenomena appear; when it vanishes, these phenomena vanish. The three worlds (that of desire, that of form and that of the formless world, i.e., the purely spiritual world) are nothing but spiritual knowledge; all phenomena are nothing but consciousness'. He was sick only when through observation he realized that the bowl was a skull; only then did his lack of concern turn into fear. Contrasts such as those between purity and impurity, peace and discord are only created by consciousness but do not exist in the objects themselves. As he realized that one could reach Enlightenment also in Korea he abandoned his journey to China and returned alone to the capital.[12]

In order to be able to refrain from value-judgments and distinctions which spring from, among other things, feelings of love and hatred, appraising what is (so-called) good and (so-called) bad, non-attachment is necessary.

LIVING ACCORDING TO ZEN

Zen practically disappeared from China. In Korea its influence has remained limited in spite of very interesting developments. It is only in Japan that, in the course of the centuries, it has become very important for the spiritual and even the daily life of the people in general.

When Zen was introduced into Japan at the beginning of the thirteenth century it was welcomed and found its followers mainly among the military caste. According to Zen one must free oneself of the limitations of logic and intellect which remain stranded in the blind alley of the contrast between subject and object and keeps man within the boundaries of birth and death. Dōgen (1200–1253), the founder of the Japanese Sōtō sect of Zen, taught that: 'It is an error to think that life passes into death. Birth is but a specific form of time which presupposes both present and past. That is why birth is also called the state of "being-unborn". It is the same with death: this, too, is based on what is gone and what is coming. Which is why it can also be called "imperishability" '.[13]

For Zen, the problem of life and death is not the question of the existence or passing away of the bodily life. And so it became the starting-point for that scorn of death, typical of the Japanese warlike caste of the *samurai* whose ideal was to be 'ego-less' (*muga*). The importance of Zen training for a *samurai* is obvious, for it taught him to suppress his own feelings and passions and to achieve 'rest in movement', a calm aloofness combined with intense action. Zen has also had much influence on some forms of art, literature and the aesthetic use of leisure (garden architecture, flower arrangement, the tea ceremony), where the point is to 'catch' the essential forms which underlie the multiplicity of the external phenomena, or to project the essence of a certain phenomenon in our context of time and space. The mental attitude acquired by the practice of Zen is also said to be the basis in principle of such sports as judo, karate and kendo.

The discovery of beauty in the severely simple, as one finds it in the architecture and the interior of the traditional Japanese home, has become a national characteristic in the course of the centuries. The appreciation of refined simplicity and the preference of merely indicating rather than reproducing the whole is not limited to these forms of art but influences social behaviour and manners.[14]

Translated by Theo Westow

Notes

1. Cf. Donald Keene, *Japanese Literature. An Introduction for Western Readers* (London, 1953), p. 39.

2. F. T. Stcherbatsky, *Buddhist Logic* II (New York, 1962), p. 32 (footnote).

3. J. J. L. Duyvendak, *Tau-te-tsjing. Het boek van weg en deugd* (Arnhem, 1950, 2nd ed.), p. 60.

4. Cf. Max Kaltenmark, *Lao Tseu et le taoïsme* (Paris, 1965), p. 55.

5. Cf. Henri Maspéro, *Le Taoïsme* (Paris 1967), pp. 40-41.

6. Cf. F. Vos & E. Zurcher, *Spel zonder snaren. Enige beschouwingen over Zen* (Deventer, 1964), pp. 87-88 and 97-98.

7. Cf. Nancy Wilson Ross, *Hinduism, Buddhism, Zen. An Introduction to Their Meaning and Their Arts* (London, 1966), p. 148.

8. Cf. Satō Kenji, *Zen no susume* (= Zen Counsels) (Tokyo, 1964), pp. 108-9; F. Vos, 'Ten Geleide', in P. Reps, *Zen-zin Zen-onzin* (Deventer, 1968).

9. He is said to have introduced Zen into China in about 500, according to the legend.

10. Cf. among others, R. H. Blyth, *Zen and Zen Classics* 4: *Mumonkan* (Tokyo, 1966), p. 71.

11. Vos & Zürcher, op. cit., p. 93.

12. Cf. Frits Vos, *Die Religionen Koreas* (Stuttgart, 1977), p. 140; Vos & Zürcher, op. cit., pp. 85-6.

13. Junyu Kitayama, *Heroisches Ethos. Das Heldische in Japan* (Berlin, 1944), p. 73.

14. See also Vos & Zürcher, op. cit., p. 196.

PART II

Theological Perspectives

Mariasusai Dhavamony

The Buddha as Saviour

THE CENTRAL figure of Buddhism is the Buddha himself whose personality captivates thousands of his followers and whose teaching arouses in them deep adherence and hope. The strong, attractive personality of the Buddha from every page of the earliest Buddhist scriptures stands out. No man was ever so godless yet so godlike, as the saying goes. Not claiming any divinity to himself, he emerged as the leader of a group of followers who pursued the 'Middle Way' between extreme asceticism and worldly life. Added to his personality, though encompassing it, there is also a conviction among Buddhists that his teaching is not only a verity but the hope of their salvation and destiny, for they recognize in his words the truth that makes slaves[1] liberated men, and different classes a common brotherhood.[2]

In such a setting of Buddhist belief and practice, important questions arise as to the nature and function of the personality of the Buddha, especially in the context of the general theme of salvation and liberation from evil and suffering. Namely, what kind of saviour was the Buddha? In the first part of this article I shall outline the personality of the Buddha, and in the second the Buddha as saviour, both from the phenomenological point of view; and in the third part I shall evaluate his saving work from the theological point of view.

THE PERSONALITY OF THE BUDDHA

Siddhārtha Gautama was born around 563 BC to the royal family of King Śuddhodana and Queen Māyā in the Śakya clan. What little appears to be authentic history is easily told. The legends of later times are mostly unreliable, though they may contain a grain of historical truth here and there. Many sermons and other pronouncements attributed to the Buddha are not his but the works of later teachers and there is also a considerable doubt about the real original message of the Buddha. We may believe as the minimum of historic truth that he was filled with the conviction that ordinary life was utterly unhappy and unsatisfactory, and that he became an ascetic in order to discover the root cause of human sorrow. After some years he succeeded in his quest to his own satisfaction and began to preach his new doctrine and to gather followers. He gained enlightenment under a sacred pipal tree at Gayā in the modern Bihar, and spent many years teaching and organizing his band of followers. He died at about the age of eighty, leaving behind him an organized community of yellow-robed monks and nuns and a basis of doctrine on which later Buddhism was built.

Siddhārtha Gautama has been given various titles or epithets. The name *Buddha* means 'enlightened' or 'awakened'. He is awakened from the sleep of ignorance and his discriminative faculty (*buddhi*) is expanded. He has been called *Bhagavat* which means 'the Lord' or 'the Blessed One'; *Jina* ('Conqueror'), *Tathāgata* ('who has come the same way'), *Sugata* ('well gone'), *Mahāpurusha* ('great person'), *Śākyamuni* ('the sage of the Śakyas'), and so on.

What kind of being was the Buddha? The answer was given by the Buddha himself. Once upon a time the brahman Dona seeing the Lord sitting at the foot of a tree and noticing the mystic marks on the Buddha's feet, asked him: 'Are you a god (*deva*)?' And the Lord answered: 'I am not'. 'Are you a celestial being (*gandharva*)?' 'I am not'. 'Are you a spiritual apparition (*yaksha*)?' 'I am not'. 'Are you a man?' 'I am not a man'. To the brahman asking him what then he might be, the answer was: 'O *brāhman*, truly I was a god, a celestial being, a spiritual apparition, a man, as long as I had not purged myself of fluxes. *Brāhmin*, just as a lotus or a water-lily born of the water . . . remains unstained by the water, even so, *brāhmin*, being born of the world . . . I remain unstained by the world. Therefore, *brāhmin*, consider me as the enlightened one'.[3]

Early Buddhist texts admit a number of deities but they live longer and in happier circumstances in the heavenly sphere than human beings; but like all other beings, they have to come down as soon as the good deeds on account of which they became gods have worn out. Even Brahmā the creator-god of Brahmanism is subject to the universal law of becoming and disappearing and hence is not exempt from birth and death.[4] It is true that in the Pāli writings Buddha is called *devātideva* ('God above gods') but this signifies that the Buddha is above the gods in the sense of having attained liberation from the cycle of rebirth and that the gods are spiritually insignificant. The highest truth and liberation cannot be obtained from the gods. Just because the Buddha has attained enlightenment, he is above all other men.

Buddhism as propounded by the Buddha does not deny the gods but recommends remembrance of them[5] only in order to recognize that they have reached their respective heavens by means of such faith, morality, and other virtues as the disciple himself possesses. They are not worshipped, they are not the basis of morality, nor are they the bestowers of happiness. While not denying their existence, Buddhism coolly deprives the conception of the deity of any value. The great Brahmā himself is reborn like any other being. He is the first to be born at the beginning of a new age, and imagines himself to be god (*iśvara*), as indeed he is for the time being. Other beings are born later, and he imagines that they have come into being at his wish, because he wished for them. And the other beings who meditate about it imagine that he is their maker, and that they themselves are impermanent and short-lived.[6] The canon represents the Buddha as visiting the Brahmā-loka; he represents himself as having received a visit from Brahmā Saham-pati; the gods, Brahmā and Indra especially, play a great part in the tradition but always in subordination to the Buddha.[7] The Buddhists really consider these gods as superior beings, though not immortal, and not differing in essence from men.

The Buddha does not exactly deny the existence of a personal God but is not really interested in him. The purpose of his doctrine is to liberate beings from suffering, and speculations concerning the origin of the world or the existence of the creator god are irrelevant. They are even a waste of time for they may prolong the life of misery by engendering ill-will in oneself and in others.

The Buddhist texts make frequent reference to the personal God (*Īśvara*) as creator of the universe and formulate clearly refutations of the doctrine that the Lord God is the creator of the universe.

Let us now determine the nature of the Buddha as enlightened or under the aspect of his glorified form. Buddhists soon saw in their master's life something of permanent and abiding value. What gave his word authority was that he had experienced the truth and attained enlightenment as the goal of salvation from the round of rebirth and suffering. When the Buddha is presented in the texts as the Seer, the Eye of the world, the Omniscient, this means that he had attained intuitive wisdom which is supreme knowledge. From the root of knowledge springs all virtue and from the root of ignorance springs all vice. The Buddha was not only a great authoritative teacher but the source of all inspiration and the fullest expression of cosmic truth.

The Buddha is the perfect man; he is the man who became a Buddha as the result of accumulated spiritual power during countless previous births and by virtue of concentrated meditation. After his enlightenment he became a supreme Teacher. He assured his disciples before his death of his continued presence with them in his teachings. He is both the supreme Teacher of the Truth that can release men from the fetters of rebirth and the supreme Example of perfect liberated man. His god-like power of omniscience, his perfection of virtues, but not creativity, all these contribute to make of him the supernormal man.

The texts speak of the bodies of the Buddha. At first, the body in which the Buddha was born, became enlightened, etc. was called the formal body (*rūpa-kāya*) and the corpus of his teachings which was the authority for the monks after his passing away was known the body of dharma (*dharma-kāya*). Later on, the formal body became two: the body of enjoyment (*sambhoga-kāya*) and the apparitional body (*nirmāna-kāya*). The *dharma-kāya* had become the cosmic body. The *nirmāna-kāya* is the body in which a Buddha appears on earth and performs the twelve acts. The *sambhoga-kāya* is the body in which he becomes fully enlightened, while his appearance on earth indicates the way of becoming a Buddha. The *dharma-kāya* comprises the five supramundane aggregates without flux: morality, concentration, insight, liberation, knowledge and the vision of liberation. The Mahayana Buddhism formulated its own doctrine of the bodies (aspects) of the Buddha eternal: the dharma body, the body of bliss and the construct body. The dharma body, the body of the eternal law, is the Buddha seen as the Absolute, omniscient, omnipotent, infinite and eternal, transcending all things. The construct body is the transcendent Buddha as incarnate in the Gautama and all other Buddhas who appear on earth from time to time. Mahāyana, however, tended to minimize the reality of the eternal Buddha's incarnation, for its teaching is that the incarnation is a mere appearance adopted by the supreme being to instruct men in the true religion and discarded when this has been realized.

Again, in the Mahāyana Sūtras (scriptures) we come across the idea of the Bodhisattva which literally means the being of enlightenment. In the early texts such a term has been used to designate the Buddha himself before he achieved illumination. The word can be rendered as Buddha designate or Buddha to be. The essential difference between Mahāyana and Theravāda Buddhism is precisely in the doctrine of the Bodhisattva who in the Mahāyana becomes a divine saviour. The Bodhisattva takes a vow not to enter into final bliss until he has saved all sentient beings; hence the solemn Bodhisattva vow:

Sentient beings are innumerable: I vow to save them all.
Defilements are inexhaustible: I vow to extinguish them all.
The doctrines of the law cannot be measured: I vow to study them.
The goal of the Buddhas is hard to reach: I vow to attain it.

Whatever the Bodhisattva thinks and acts is determined by compassion (*karuṇā*): 'The Bodhisattva . . . need not train himself in too many virtues (*dharma*). To one virtue . . . (however) the Bodhisattva has to devote himself, he has to hold it in honour (for) through it all Buddha virtues become evident. Which is this one virtue? It is great compassion'. The Bodhisattva is a being intent on enlightenment, one who has experienced suffering in his own life and arouses compassion for sentient beings who suffer and aspires to allay their suffering. We can sum up in the following points what Buddhists believe with respect to the being and nature of the Buddha. In Theravāda Buddhism, the historical Buddha is regarded as a perfect man, the most honoured elder brother of mankind (*jettho settho lokassa*), and as supernormal being or superman because of his having attained enlightenment. In the Mahāyāna he is interpreted as the projection or manifestation of the Absolute. He is in essence with ultimate being but an illusion in his frail mortal frame.

Very early in the history of Buddhism a sort of the Buddhist confession of faith in the three jewels was formulated by the monks: 'I take refuge in the Buddha; I take refuge in the doctrine (*dharma*); I take refuge in the *sangha* (order or community)'. We easily understand why such an act of faith is taken with respect to the Doctrine and the Order of monks. But why faith in the Buddha, if he was not God? The reason is that the Buddha was no longer a man, no longer a person, an individual. Though his body had perished and his personality had dissolved in *nirvana,* yet monks and laymen 'took refuge' in him. This only shows that by the time the formula of the three jewels was established Buddhism has become a popular religion and not just a system of mental and spiritual training.

A modern educated Buddhist, when he reveres the image of the Buddha and places flowers in his shrine, explains that he believes in the Buddha as the great teacher of the truth and that he embodies the truth or doctrine. But a simple lay believer will tend to look on the Buddha as the greatest of the divinities, and on *nirvana* as the permanent 'heaven'. And this is true even of the Theravāda sect. The monks were not slow to grasp the felt need of the simple folk for worship and to cater to their spontaneous sentiment and expression of venerating the Buddha. Thus in every Buddhist monastery (*vihāra*) there is a *stupa*, a hemispherical mound usually faced with stone and containing a relic casket, round which both monks and laymen solemnly walk in clockwise direction reverencing the Buddha while doing so. The *stupa* reminds the believer of the Buddha's final entry into *nirvana* (his death). In a similar way the pipal tree which is also circumambulated with reverence symbolizes his enlightenment. The image of the Buddha himself is a third religious symbol in Buddhism. The image of the Buddha is placed in a shrine-room before which the laymen prostrated themselves and offered flowers, as if to a Hindu deity.

THE BUDDHA AS SAVIOUR

What does a Buddhist mean by salvation or liberation? It is extremely important to understand this notion in order to have a proper understanding of Buddhism itself. The nature of the Buddha's original teaching is contained in the 'sermon of the turning of the wheel of the law', which is said to be the first discourse of the Buddha after his enlightenment. It does not refer to God or gods, and makes no mention of the soul. The sermon contains the following points. There are two ends not to be served by a wanderer—the pursuit of desires and of the pleasure which springs from desires, which is base, common, ignoble, and unprofitable; and the pursuit of pain and hardship which is grievous, ignoble and unprofitable. The middle way avoids both these ends. It brings clear vision, it makes for wisdom, and leads to peace, insight, enlightenment and *nirvana*. The four noble truths are that of sorrow, that of the arising of sorrow, that of the stopping of sorrow, and finally that of the way which leads to the stopping of sorrow; this way consists of an eightfold path: right views, right resolve, right speech, right conduct, right livelihood, right effort, right mindfulness, and right concentration. This is the middle way.

Now the concept of *nirvana* is a difficult one; and according to the Pāli texts, the Buddha himself never clearly defined it, for it is indescribable, a state which can only be understood from personal experience. We can describe it as a condition in which all clinging and craving have vanished forever, where the specious personality has dissolved, which is neither being nor non-being but transcending both. It is extinction from the fire of passion, from the fire of illusion, when pride, false views, and the lusts and pains are extinguished. 'The wise man who, firmly standing on morality, cultivates consciousness and insight, he the monk ardent and prudent, may disentangle this tangle'. In other words *nirvana* means the lifting of the burden of the personality and a profound sense of spiritual freedom, of release from the bondage of rebirth and sorrow.

This much in the Theravāda. *Nirvana* for the Mahāyāna means the becoming conscious of one's own absoluteness and is a state of mental aloofness from, but within, the world which includes active endeavour for the liberation of other beings. Man in his intimate essence possesses the Buddha nature and has only to become aware of this reality through morality and meditation. To partake of the Buddha nature means not only to share in the timeless bliss of *nirvana* but also to have a part in the Buddha's own boundless wisdom, compassion and love.

In brief, the Buddha's great discovery is that all suffering in the world is ultimately rooted in thirst for life, attachment to existence. The facts of suffering and of death wherever there is life and the possibility of escape from all the three for all sentient beings, as we know, are the corner stones of Buddhism. Buddhist salvation in its negative aspect means liberation from suffering and rebirth and in its positive aspect means attainment of *nirvana*, understood differently by different sects; namely either as a state of highest bliss, peace, something absolute as opposed to the process of continuous change, or the realization of the Buddha-wisdom and the becoming of the Buddha. The early statements on enlightenment explain it as follows: The Buddha is said to have methodically fixed his mind on the thought: 'This is suffering . . . knowledge (*jñāna*) arose, vision (*cakṣus*) arose, wisdom (*vidyā*) arose, discrimination (*buddhi*) arose, intelligence arose, insight (*prajñā*) arose, light arose'. He saw the *dharma;* 'he who sees the *dharma* sees me, and he who sees me sees the *dharma*'.[8] Later Mahāyāna texts understand by enlightenment insight into the meaning of *dharma*, of dependent origination and of the *tathāgata*. The Buddha is seen as dharma. The Buddha is said to have experienced three kinds of wisdom (*vidyā*) in the three watches of the night in which he attained complete enlightenment: the knowledge of his previous births; the knowledge of the passing away and rebirth of sentient beings, seeing with a divine eye, surpassing the human, the beings passing on to various destinies according to their motivated actions; and the knowledge of the destruction of the fluxes, the defiling elements.

It is in such a setting of the doctrine of salvation that we have to understand how the Buddha is considered a saviour by the Buddhists.

First the Buddha is saviour of mankind for the Buddhists in so far as he is the teacher of the saving truth or doctrine. 'Just, O Brethren, as the wide sea has but one taste, the taste of salt, so also, Brethren, have this Doctrine and Discipline one only taste, the taste of Salvation'.[9] No one else has seen and realized the supreme truth except the Buddha. Hence the Buddha is indispensable to know this truth. In this connection we have to note that he was not a social reformer except indirectly and in the secondary sense which can be said of all religious teachers. Nor was he a teacher of philosophy, for time and again he insists on his disinterest in metaphysics and refuses to answer the questions on the origin of the world, of the existence of God and of the nature of the Absolute. 'It is, Brethren, as if a man were pierced through by a poisoned arrow, and his friends, companions, and near relatives called in a surgeon, and he should say, ''I will not have this arrow pulled out until I know who the man is that has wounded me; whether he is of the royal caste or of the priests' caste, a citizen or a servant''; or else he should say, ''I will not have his arrow pulled until I know who the man is that has wounded me whether he is tall or short, or of medium height'' '.[10] The Buddha then considered himself as a physician-teacher who had a practical cure to offer men. The doctrine he gave is the cure for the spiritually sick men in order that they be freed from suffering and rebirth. He has only found the spiritual cure but every man must rely on his own effort principally to attain liberation.

The Buddha as teacher is present in the doctrine itself which he had left for posterity. 'He who sees the teaching (doctrine) he is he who sees the teacher'.[11] Again the Buddha says: 'Whosoever shall turn to me with faith and love—he shall reach the heaven-world. And whatsoever monks shall conform themselves to the teaching, walking in full faith—these shall attain to the full awakening'.[12] No doubt, devotion to the teacher will carry one far; but obedience to his teaching alone will make one reach *nirvana*. He taught his followers to make an effort to follow the austere doctrine at all cost: 'He who is near me, yet is covetous, lustful, and malevolent is far from me'.[13]

The Buddha not only taught the saving doctrine but set a powerful example. He exemplified to his followers a living truth, a dynamic wisdom, and an active compassion. Such a lofty teaching without the powerful example of his life would have resulted in mere nothing and despair. In this aspect the Buddha presents himself as a saviour and rightly so. Of Gautama's serenity, of his moral earnestness, of his sweet reasonableness, of his compassion, of his wisdom, and above all of his power to win followers and influence people, there can be no doubt, for the early Buddhist writings portray him as supreme model to be imitated upon. Gautama's fame is most tellingly depicted thus: 'This is he, the holy one, the perfect in knowledge and in conduct, the auspicious, the knower of all the worlds, the incomparable trainer of men that wish to be trained, the teacher of gods and men, the awakened one, the holy one . . . He proclaims the truth, excellent in its inception, its progress, its culmination, according to the spirit and to the letter. He preaches the holy life, perfect and pure. Blessed it is to be old such an exalted one'.[14] Also because of these reasons he had been endowed by some with the divine attributes such as omniscience, saving power, timeless existence, unending bliss, immutable existence, and so on.

To the Theravādins the historical Buddha is only the teacher of the truth and the historicity of the Buddha itself is of little consequence in comparison with the eternal truth manifested by innumerable Buddhas throughout the ages. Thus a clear distinction is made between the teacher and the doctrine or truth, and even the effort to practise the doctrine conduces to salvation. But for the Mahāyānists the Buddha, the awakened one, is the concrete realization of the truth which cannot be reduced to any clear-cut formula. The Buddha is primarily a religious fact, a presence in the world, which may be explained by diverse philosophies but never wholly comprehended.

It is in this Mahāyānist perspective that we have to understand how the Bodhisattva becomes a suffering saviour. The Bodhisattva makes the solemn resolve at the beginning of his career: namely, not only resolves to pity and help all mortal beings, but also to share their suffering. 'All creatures are in pain'. The Bodhisattva resolves, 'all suffer from bad and hindering *karma* . . . so that they cannot see the Buddhas or hear the Law of righteousness or know the Order . . . All that mass of pain and evil *karma* I take in my own body . . . I take upon myself the burden of sorrow; I resolve to do so; I endure it all. I do not turn back or run away, I do not tremble . . . I am not afraid nor do I despair. Assuredly I must bear the burdens of all beings . . . for I have resolved to save them all. I must set them all free, I must save the whole world from the forest of birth, old age, disease, and rebirth, from misfortune and sin, from the round of birth and death, from the toils of heresy. For all beings are caught in the net of craving, encompassed by ignorance, held by the desire for existence; they are doomed to destruction, shut in a cage of pain . . . they are ignorant, untrustworthy, full of doubts, always at loggerheads one with another, always prone to see evil; they cannot find a refuge in the ocean of existence; they are all on the edge of the gulf of destruction. I work to establish the kingdom of perfect wisdom for all beings. I care not at all for my own deliverance. I must save all beings from the torrent of rebirth with the raft of my omniscient mind. I must pull them back from the great precipice. I must free them from all misfortunes, ferry them over the stream of rebirth'.[15] According to the Theravāda, one could save oneself only by one's own personal effort; 'none could be saved by another'. But in the Mahāyāna this attitude of exclusive self-reliance is undermined. In this sect a large number of saviours are admitted and there is also the transfer of merit from the Bodhisattva to the believers; and the salvation consists in realizing the Buddha nature that is found in every man. As the Mahāyāna text says: 'To turn over or to dedicate their merit to the enlightenment of all beings'. 'Through the merit derived from all my good deeds I wish to appease the suffering of all creatures, to be the medicine, the physician, and the nurse of the sick as long as there is sickness. Through rains of food and drink I wish to extinguish the fire of hunger and thirst. I wish to be an inexhaustible treasure to the poor, a servant who furnishes them with all they lack. My life and all my rebirth, all my possessions, all the merit that I have acquired or will acquire, all that I abandon without hope of any gain for myself in order that the salvation of all beings might be promoted'. The point is that the transfer of merit is carried out by the Bodhisattva in the last stages of his spiritual ascendency. The part of great spiritual merit is transferred to the believer if he asks for it in faith. The attitude of faith (*saddha*) of which there is question here means in the Buddhist context serene and glad confidence that all is well, because the teaching is true and the teacher is infallible and implies the belief that the Bodhisattva is powerful to effect the saving influence on others when they are resorted to. The words *pasāda, cittapasāda,* and *manopasāda* are frequently used in the sense of faith in the Buddha or Bodhisattva, as the case may be, literally signifying rejoicing because of the joy or peace of mind which faith in the Buddha or in the Bodhisattva brings with it.

THEOLOGICAL REFLECTIONS

Now we consider the above-mentioned points of Buddhist salvation and of the Buddha as saviour of mankind in the light of Christian faith and evaluate their salvific merit, for the theology of world religions means precisely this and makes use of Christian revelation and faith as criteria of judgment.

First, Christianity has always been faith in Christ and his saving message, seeking an understanding of its doctrine. It centres upon the person of Christ, the God-man, and faith in him and his salvific efficacy. On the contrary Buddhism is first of all a doctrine, a wisdom, which generates faith in the doctrine. The Buddha handed over to posterity a sublime doctrine and it is because of this that a Buddhist expresses his faith in the Buddha. Respect, reverence, veneration of an 'elder brother of mankind', as the Buddha was called, of a great teacher because of the intrinsic merit of his teaching, and because of the wonderful example that he showed in the way of realizing concretely what he taught, relate the believer to the person of the Buddha. This relationship of the believer to the Buddha is based on the conviction that the Buddha is not God but a superman, or the perfect enlightened being. Even for Mahāyanist believers, the Buddha is the concrete realization of the doctrine and the Buddha is considered to be present in the doctrine.

To a Buddhist history is of little consequence in comparison to the eternal doctrine that is time and again manifested by innumerable Buddhas throughout the ages. Even when the focus is put on the historical Buddha, and the historical Buddha is an actual religious fact, it is his glorified status or enlightened form of being that is essential to the Buddhist faith. On the contrary the fact of Christ's appearance in time and the historicity of Christ-event, of the sayings and the doings of Christ form the essential part of the Christian message.

Buddhism is based neither on a revelation *of* God nor on a revelation *from* God. Its beginning is ascribed to a human reality, the Buddha for whom the reality of God is of no concern; hence there is no question of any intervention of God in human history or of divinely revealed truths in Buddhism. Buddhism starts from an experience of the human condition, an insight into the essential structure of the phenomenal existence and an effort to transcend the state of man in his misery and suffering.

Both for the Buddha and for the Buddhists there can be no Personal God who creates the world and governs it. Hence the experience of *nirvana* or the realization of the Buddhahood is interpreted as an escape from the instability of the world and of phenomenal existence in general. From the Buddhist point of view there is no God of history or salvation history. Both the experience of *nirvana* and the realization of the Buddhahood are certainly suggestive of an absolute or transcendent state, something like the divine in other religions; but they entail complete dissociation from and disgust with the world of suffering, of birth and rebirth. This vision in some sects is counterbalanced by compassion for all sentient beings which sets the wheel of the Buddhist dharma in motion, by means of which man can be saved. Salvation means liberation from the round of existence, from ignorance and suffering and not salvation and sanctification *of* the world, for the world is in a state of continuous flux, subject to disquiet. Moreover salvation is not liberation from morally evil or sin in the Christian sense of the world.

Since without the Buddha's teaching no man can come to know of the eightfold noble path, we must conclude that the Buddha is saviour of mankind in this sense. Namely, the Buddha alone discovered the saving truth. Moreover the stories of the Buddha's life and the presence of his image are certainly appealing to the Buddhists and thus evoke in them a religious feeling of faith, devotion. We have to note that the question of 'helping' or 'saving' others is presented specifically as a question of teaching: i.e., of sharing enlightenment. In this sense he is not merely a teacher and saviour but also an image of saving inspiration for the practice of the Buddhist way of liberation. The highest possible degree of help that the Buddha could offer to his followers along the way of salvation is his life and example which is the concrete manifestation of the Doctrine he taught. We cannot say that the Buddha is the incarnation of the ultimate reality in time and space. For the Buddha is not *nirvana* incarnate, for *nirvana* is not a divine principle or Person seeking to save the lost and sinful man. The Buddha is neither God nor embodiment or manifestation of God. The faithful revere the memory of the Buddha as a supreme teacher and example.

The basic act of taking refuge with the three jewels, the Buddha, *dharma*, and *saṅgha* involves a certain amount of faith experience and invites devotion and piety from the believers. Essentially, it means trust in the efficacy of the doctrine which the Buddha alone discovered and taught. The figure of the suffering Bodhisattva is very appealing; but in the compassionate Bodhisattva the ultimate reality is the contemplative insight of 'emptiness' and is not at all a personal God.

Buddhism in its various forms is profoundly conscious of the basic insufficiency of this world and teaches men to escape from it. The way enables the Buddhists to reach either a state of perfect liberation or supreme illumination when they make serious whole-hearted effort to follow it in faith, whether they rely on their own strength or on help from on high. The Buddha is the perfect embodiment of this Doctrine and had shown the way to liberation. It is along these basic intuitions of Buddhism that we find many valid moral and religious values; and in so far as they are genuinely true and noble, and in so far as they help us to penetrate into the personality of the Buddha himself as saviour, they also present themselves as efficacious helps or ways of penetrating into the mystery of Christ and of understanding the Christian mystery of salvation.

Notes

1. Namely, slaves of passion and desire, of flux and impermanence, of suffering and the cycle of rebirths.

2. Different classes of men are primarily to be understood in the sense of Indian caste system, and then in the wider sense of race or national groups.

3. *Anguttara Nikāya*, 2.37-38.

4. *Anguttara Nikāya*, 10.29.

5. *Anguttara Nikāya*, 3.287. This is one of the subjects of meditation called the six remembrances (*anussati*): the Buddha, the Doctrine, the Order, morality, liberality, and the gods.

6. See *Brahmajāla-sutta*.

7. *Majjhima Nikāya*, 1.326; 458.

8. *Samyutata Nikāya*, 3.120; *Itivuttaka*, 91.

9. *Cullavagga*, IX.

10. *Majjhima Nikāya*, 1.8.

11. *Theragāthā*, CCV.

12. *Discourses of Gautama Buddha*, translated by Sīlacāra 1, p. 181.

13. *Itivuttaka*, cited by K. J. Saunders, *Gotama Buddha* (Madras, 1955), pp. 73-74.

14. *Discourses of Gautama Buddha*, 11, p. 152.

15. *Śikṣāsamuccaya*, pp. 278ff.

Maha Sthavira Sangharakshita

Dialogue between Buddhism and Christianity

BUDDHISM AND CHRISTIANITY

BUDDHISM and Christianity are universal religions. They are not, like the old ethnic religions, limited to a particular part of the earth's surface or to a particular breeding-group within the human population, nor, strictly speaking, is it possible to be born into them. Although for purposes of communication they adopted—in fact had to adopt—the outward forms of the culture (Vedic-Sramanic and Judaeo-Hellenic respectively) in the midst of which they originally appeared, and although they subsequently gave birth to distinctive cultures of their own, neither of them can be identified with even the most highly developed culture; nor can they, with justice, be discussed in exclusively 'cultural' terms. In principle, the message of both Buddhism and Christianity is addressed not to man as a member of a group (family, tribe, and so on) but to man as an individual who is capable of responding as an individual and either of attaining *nirvana*, realizing Buddhahood, and so on, or of saving his own soul, winning the Kingdom of Heaven, and so on. An individual becomes a Buddhist, or becomes a Christian, in the one case through the act of going for refuge to the Three Jewels (Buddha, Dharma, Sangha), in the other by undergoing the rite of baptism. Those who have gone for refuge, or who have been baptized, form a spiritual community (*sangha*, church) that is in reality quite distinct from any mundane group to which a Buddhist or a Christian may also belong even when all the other members of that group happen to be Buddhists or Christians.

Although Buddhism and Christianity are both universal religions,

55

and although as universal religions they resemble each other more closely than they resemble any of the ethnic religions, they are, at the same time, about as different from each other as it is possible for them to be. One might in fact say, paradoxically, that it is possible for them to be so different just because they are both universal religions. The differences between them are both intrinsic and extrinsic. Buddhism is not only non-theistic, but the most important representative of the non-theistic group of religions, to which also belong ethnic religions like Taoism and Confucianism, as well as Jainism, which even though it has remained confined to the Indian sub-continent is in principle a universal religion. Christianity is of course theistic, and the principal representative of the theistic group of religions, which includes Judaism, which is an ethnic religion, and Islam, which is a universal religion with strong ethnic features. In fact, on account of its subtle and complex Trinitarian doctrine Christianity may be considered the theistic religion *par excellence*.

On the practical side, Buddhism emphasises the importance of the part played by meditation and contemplation (*śamatha* and *vipaśyanā*) in spiritual development, whereas Christianity insists on the indispensability of the sacraments for the living of the Christian life. In profane historical-phenomenological terms, Christianity is the principal Semitic faith, Buddhism the leading Indo-Aryan teaching. Christianity has dominated the history of Europe, while Buddhism has profoundly influenced the history of Asia. Christianity is the religion of the West. Buddhism is the religion of the East.

Despite the fact that these two great spiritual phenomena grew up in the same world—indeed, occupied opposite ends of the same great Eurasian land mass—until very recent times there was no real contact between them. Nestorian Christians and Mahayana Buddhists did, of course, have a certain amount of contact in Central Asia, perhaps in China too; a life of the Buddha found its way into mediaeval Europe as the biography of a Christian saint; Desideri made his way to Lhasa, and wrote a book in Tibetan in which he refuted Buddhism, and St Francis Xavier argued with a Zen monk—and that was about all. Only in very recent times has there been anything like sustained or significant contact between the two religions, and as time goes on such contact is likely to increase rather than diminish. Indeed, it can be expected to play an ever more important part in the spiritual life of mankind.

THE NATURE OF DIALOGUE

According to the dictionary, a dialogue is a conversation between two people. It might therefore be expected that a dialogue between

Buddhism and Christianity would be simply a conversation, in the sense of an exchange of views, between the two religions. But in fact this is not so. In the modern 'ecumenical' context—whether as between sects within one and the same religion or as between different religions—the term dialogue has come to possess not only a more specialized but a richer meaning. This meaning is not unconnected with the fact that many of the sects and religions that are nowadays parties to dialogue, but especially the religions, have hitherto developed in complete isolation. This is particularly so, as we have seen, in the case of Buddhism and Christianity, which for by far the greater part of their careers have remained in almost total ignorance of each other's existence. Because they developed in mutual isolation, and because they moreover met with no decisive spiritual challenge from any other universal religion, both Buddhism and Christianity tended to see themselves as religious absolutes, within whose all-embracing synthesis a place, and an explanation, could be found for all the spiritual facts of existence—including, in theory at least, the teachings of all other religions.

In this respect the position which the two religions adopted on the spiritual plane (and on the earthly plane too, in the case of the mediaeval Papacy) was analogous to the position adopted on the sociological plane by the civilizations of ancient India and ancient China. Jambudvipa was synonymous with the inhabited earth, the Middle Kingdom equivalent to the whole civilized world. When China, in the middle of the last century, first came in contact with the western powers, it was forced to recognize that these were not, in fact, outlying dependencies of the Celestial Empire that could be overawed by a few well-chosen words from the Dragon Throne, but independent sovereign states with whom she was obliged to treat on equal terms. In much the same way, Buddhism and Christianity have been brought face to face, and forced to recognize each other's existence as separate spiritual universes. Christianity can no longer put Buddhism in its place, as it were, by speaking of it as a mere ethical system, or as a form of natural mysticism. Buddhism can no longer relate Christianity to the *devayana* with a good-natured comment on the spiritual inadequacies of theism. From now onwards Buddhism and Christianity must take each other more seriously than that. Henceforth they must try to communicate.

But for communication to be possible there must be a medium of communication; there must be a common language. Since the two religions developed in complete independence of each other, however, no such common language exists. Both of them developed, of course, a powerful and flexible 'theological' or 'Buddhological' language which is as adequate to the expression of their own ultimate content (divine revelation, enlightenment) as a language of this sort can by its very nature be, but in each case the language is completely understandable—or fully 'transparent'—only to the members of the spiritual community within which it arose and who habitually use it as their means of communication with one another. What is said in one 'language' cannot be translated into the other without very serious distortion. Even to speak in terms of 'Buddhology', as though there was something in Buddhism corresponding to the Christian notion of theology—even, in fact, to speak of Buddhism as a religion—is already to introduce an element of distortion into the discussion. There is also no question of Buddhism and Christianity alike being translated into some neutral (?) 'universalist' Esperanto and then left to communicate with each other through this medium. Were this to be done, the possibility of distortion, and therefore of mutual incomprehension, would be increased to such an extent that even if communication were achieved it could hardly be regarded as a communication between Buddhism and Christianity. Having been brought face to face, and forced to recognize each other's existence, Buddhism and Christianity are in the position of having to communicate without a medium of communication, without a common language. In the ecumenical context, it is in this communication without a medium of communication, that the essence of dialogue consists. Less paradoxically, dialogue is that form of communication in which the means of communication has to be created in the course of the process of communication itself.

THE PRINCIPAL OBSTACLE TO DIALOGUE

Obstacles to a fruitful dialogue between Buddhism and Christianity are of many kinds. Even in these days of improved communications, Buddhists and Christians may not always find it easy to meet. There may be difficulties arising out of the special nature of one's vocation, whether as parish priest, meditation master, or social worker. Moreover, the members of one's flock, or one's religious superiors, may not approve of contact between the followers of the two religions. Even when one is face to face with one's partner in dialogue there are still psychological obstacles to be surmounted. Suspicion and prejudice enter only too easily into any human heart, and one may at times be deficient in honesty, in patience, in charity (*maitrī*), and even in common courtesy. More formidable still, there is the inherent difficulty of grasping the real meaning of concepts with which one is totally unfamiliar, as well as of appreciating the significance of symbols that one finds strange and even bizarre. But the principal obstacle to fruitful dialogue consists in confusing dialogue with certain other activities which, though they superficially resemble it, are really quite different. Dialogue can be confused with discussion, with debate, and with diplomacy. Above all, it can be confused with monologue. As long as this confusion persists, no dialogue is possible. Indeed, by creating the illusion of dialogue when, in fact, no dialogue is taking place, it actually postpones the achievement of dialogue indefinitely.

The nature of discussion, debate and diplomacy is not difficult to understand. For our present purpose, discussion may be defined as the exchanging of ideas, debate as arguing for victory, and diplomacy as the strategy by which a pseudo-religious power structure seeks to ensure its own survival and aggrandizement, and the destruction of its competitors, by secular means other than that of open violence. A discussion between Buddhism and Christianity, or between Buddhists and Christians, differs from a dialogue in its being conducted, more often than not, on an abstract, not to say an academic, basis, and in its not going deep enough to come up against the fact that they are speaking two different languages and are not, in fact, really intelligible to each other. Similarly, a debate differs from a dialogue inasmuch as because both religions see themselves as absolutes neither victory or defeat is possible for either. Debate is thus based on a false assumption. As for diplomacy, this is, in reality, not a form of religious activity at all, but arises only to the extent that on its 'institutional' side a religion has, under 'ethnic' influence, sunk from being a spiritual community (*sangha,* church) to being a secular group among secular groups, that is to say, a political and/or socio-economic power structure among power structures.

Since the broad sense in which discussion, debate, and diplomacy are not dialogue is obvious enough, nothing more need be said about them. But in what sense of the term, exactly, is monologue not dialogue? Apart from the purely formal opposition between the two terms, this is not so obvious, and because it is not so obvious, and because it is the confusion of dialogue with monologue, in particular, that is the principal obstacle to dialogue, in this case a few words of explanation are required. As we have already seen, both Buddhism and Christianity tend to see themselves as religious absolutes. Each is a universe in itself. Each speaks its own theological or 'Buddhological' language, as it were, and what is said in one language cannot really be translated into the other. In communicating with each other, therefore, both religions are likely to be misunderstood. This may not always be realized. In fact, both parties may be under the impression that they are communicating, and that dialogue is taking place, when this is not so at all. What has happened is that A has taken a word, or a concept, used by B, has attached to it the meaning that it bears for A, and then replied to B as though B had used it in the sense which it would have had for A had A used it. A is therefore not replying to something that B has said but to something that A has said. A is therefore not communicating with B at all. A is communicating with A. What is taking place is not a dialogue but a monologue. Buddhism, for example, may attach to the word God, as used by Christianity, the same meaning that it is accustomed to associate with its own Mahabrahma, and may try to continue the communication on those terms. Similarly, Christianity may attach to such words as voidness (*śunyatā*), trance (*dhyāna*), and Wisdom (*prajñā*), meanings quite different from those which they traditionally hold for Buddhism. Misunderstandings of this sort are much less likely to arise—or if they do arise much more likely to be corrected—when the two religions meet in the persons of an individual Buddhist and an individual Christian, communicating in the flesh. When they meet only on paper, with the Buddhist or the Christian author trying to communicate with a Christianity or a Buddhism that exists nowhere but in his own brain the result will be not dialogue but monologue.

THE PROBABLE BEST METHOD OF STARTING DIALOGUE

If dialogue is not confused with discussion, debate or diplomacy, and if Buddhism and Christianity meet in the persons of an individual Buddhist and an individual Christian, the question of the best method of starting dialogue can probably be left to look after itself. Provided that the two parties to the dialogue are open to each other, and provided each really listens to what the other has to say, there is no reason why dialogue should not take place—no reason why they should not be able to communicate even without a medium of communication: that is, without a common language, without a mutually acceptable system of concepts, symbols, and values. When dialogue takes place, however, both parties should realize that it is bound to be of a very piecemeal nature, and that they should not expect too much from it. Indeed, they should not expect anything at all from it except the possibility of continued dialogue. If they expect an accession of interesting new ideas, it will become discussion. If they expect victory, or even just the enrichment of, or a positive contribution to, their own (Buddhist or Christian) religious experience, it will become debate. If they expect an accommodation with regard to the practical interests of the secular power structure with which, on their 'institutional' side, they may happen to be identified, it becomes diplomacy.

More important than the question of the best method of starting dialogue is that of the best person to start it. The 'what?' is at bottom a 'who?'. In deciding who is the best person, however, we must be careful not to overlook the obvious fact that a dialogue between Buddhism and Christianity is a dialogue between Buddhism and Christianity. It is a dialogue, that is to say, between these two religions in their central, 'classical' forms—not a dialogue between them in any diluted, demythologized, rationalized and secularized, modern version. Buddhism and Christianity can, in fact, engage in dialogue only in the persons of a fully committed Buddhist and a firmly believing Christian, and it is these, therefore, who are the best persons to start—and carry on—dialogue between the two religions. On no account can Buddhist-Christian dialogue be regarded as a fashionable exercise for an uncommitted academic, or for those Buddhists or Christians who, uncertain of their own faith, are looking for an intellectually stimulating and professionally rewarding career in the field of 'comparative' religious studies. This does not mean that those who engage in dialogue may not be equipped with a scientific knowledge of Buddhism or of Christianity as, for example, a sociological phenomenon. It means that a scientific knowledge of a religion is not, in itself, a qualification for engaging in dialogue on its behalf.

RELIGIOUS EXPERIENCE CHARACTERISTIC OF BUDDHISM AS A STARTING-POINT IN DIALOGUE WITH BUDDHISM?

From the Christian point of view, it would seem that the religious experience characteristic of Buddhism is quite acceptable as a starting-point in dialogue with Buddhism. But even if not taken as an actual starting-point, once dialogue had really begun the subject of religious experience could hardly fail to be brought up sooner or later (presumably it would also be possible to take 'religious experience as characteristic of Christianity' as a starting-point in dialogue with Buddhism). From the Buddhist point of view, however, the expression 'religious experience' is ambiguous and, therefore, misleading. It could, for instance, be taken to refer either to the experience of concentration and meditation (sámathā), or to the experience of insight (vipaśyanā); to the act of going for refuge to the Three Jewels, to the arising of the Bodhichitta, or to the 'turning about' (paravṛtti) in the deepest seat (āśraya) of consciousness (vijñāna). Even if it is taken in the restricted sense of the experience of suffering, and we focus attention on that, serious objections can still be raised against the taking of religious experience as characteristic of Buddhism as a starting point in dialogue at all. Indeed, the identification of 'religious experience' with the experience of suffering and liberation from suffering may serve to reinforce these objections.

Whatever form of communication we engage in, progress is from the simple to the complex, from the shallow to the profound, the peripheral to the central. This is all the more so in the case of the form of communication we call dialogue, wherein religious absolutes confront each other without the benefit of a common language. It would therefore appear that for Christianity to take religious experience as characteristic of Buddhism, especially the experience of liberation from suffering, as a starting point in dialogue with Buddhism, is not really feasible. Indeed, by coming to premature conclusions about the nature of this experience it might even make dialogue between the two religions impossible. Religious experience is an extremely difficult thing to communicate, even when a medium of communication exists, and the experience of liberation from suffering is not an 'experience' in the ordinary sense, not even a 'religious experience'. For Buddhism it is not just liberation from ordinary human wretchedness, but from everything conditioned (saṁskṛta) and mundane (laukika). As such, it is identical with the attainment of Nirvana or Enlightenment (bodhi) or, in other words, with the ultimate goal of Buddhism—a goal that must be realized by one's personal spiritual exertions and which is, we are expressly told, beyond the sphere of reasoning (attakka-vācara).

This brings us to a second ambiguity, not one of language but identity. When religious experience as characteristic of Buddhism is put forward as a possible starting point in dialogue with Buddhism, it is not clear whose religious experience is meant. Is it the experience of the Buddhist who is party to the dialogue? (I assume, perhaps wrongly, that his Christian counterpart will have no Buddhist religious experience). Or is it the experience of some other Buddhist, living or dead, who does not himself actually participate in dialogue? Is it, even, not any particular person's experience at all that is meant, but some general concept of religious experience—a concept which, so far as any actual parties to Buddhist-Christian dialogue are concerned, may be no more than a matter of words? These questions are raised, not in any hair-splitting spirit of pedantry, much less still in order to make dialogue more difficult, but simply as a means of emphasizing the fact that the starting-point of dialogue with Buddhism should be something about which at least one of the two parties can speak from personal knowledge. There is a world of difference between taking religious experience as characteristic of Buddhism as a starting point in dialogue and taking as starting point the words and concepts which traditionally reflect that experience.

In view of these facts it would therefore appear that some more peripheral topic than 'religious experience', or the experience of liberation from suffering, is needed as a starting-point for dialogue with

Buddhism; that is, some point of doctrine, or religious practice, or liturgical observance, that is intelligible to, and within the imaginative grasp of, both parties. Religion need not be identified exclusively with 'religious experience'. Indeed, the exaggerated value which is sometimes attached to religious experience in the narrower, more subjective sense, is not a feature of Buddhism, and to give any impression to the contrary would be to misrepresent Buddhism. Even if, for some reason, religious experience as characteristic of Buddhism has to be taken as a starting point in dialogue with Buddhism, there can be no question of anyone embarking on a confident exposition of that about which even the Enlightened hesitate to speak. Rather should some more modest, everyday type of religious experience be taken as a starting point. If this is done, and if on both sides there is sufficient openness and sufficient awareness of their own limitations, then there may be some hope that a truly fruitful dialogue will begin between Buddhism and Christianity: that is, a dialogue that will not degenerate into monologue but continue.

Dominique Dubarle

Buddhist Spirituality and the Christian Understanding of God

BUDDHISM is not really a religion in the Western meaning of the term. Its spiritual attitudes and rules of conduct often approach what the West would call religious, with an intensity and purity that can well serve us as examples, but it seems to me that one should be as wary of too rapid an assimilation as of over-hasty suppositions of difference. Human affairs, even the less profound and essential aspects of them, cannot be treated in a simplistic way. Where possible, it is better to allow for the play of a certain osmosis in life and to try patiently to recognize from within what this is in the process of teaching us.

In dealing with Buddhism, whatever form it takes (and there are very many of them), I believe one should always start from the experience of the Buddha before his illumination: the experience of what Buddhism itself calls *dukkha*. It is, however, important to recognize that this word designates an experience which western vocabulary cannot adequately define. We can say: 'sorrow, pain, the misery of life'—yes, it does mean these things but it also means inconsistency, disillusion, vanity: something approaching what the biblical author of Ecclesiastes had in mind. It also designates a certain mode of unhappy enslavement, unconscious at the beginning but becoming conscious and as though perched on the edge of a deep abyss of unconsciousness surrounded by a glimmer of awakening, arousing an intense desire for liberation.

The special, cultural accompaniments of Buddhism should also be borne in mind. First, the idea of *karma* which so strongly denotes the feeling of the fatal involvement of being in its acts and their infinite prolonging. This is in a way only an intellectualized working-out of the

64

experience of *dukkha*. Even earlier, Indian thought produced the theory of existence evoked by the word *saṃsāra:* the limitless cycle of future reincarnations of the mental being exposed once more to the *dukkha* of existence and pursuing the fulfilment of *karma*.[1]

Dukkha, karma, saṃsāra: despite everything, liberation is possible; man's task is to win it, to pass over to the farther shore of life. Absolutely, in a way that involves his whole being and which questions the totality of what we call the world. The Buddha experienced the conquest of this liberation with an unequalled intensity, experiencing what he came to call 'illumination', and he preached the good news of this with extraordinarily persuasive power. The great texts of traditional Buddhist teaching—and these texts amount to a very few—are among the most powerful in the world with their ability to move in one way or another, even a western way, anyone who has acquired a sensitivity to what the word *dukkha* comes to mean for the Buddhist mind. This applies even when the feeling of *karma* or the teaching of *saṃsāra* do not have the same hold over the mind that they can well have in the native context of Buddhism.

It is just at this point that a Christian—at least the Christian of the sort that I am—begins to mistrust hasty dialogues and even well-intentioned approaches.

Spiritual communication, if there is such a thing possible (of which I am convinced), is very difficult to embody in our language. It seems to me hardly possible to get somewhere near truth except by using a sort of ranging method, saying probably excessive things in one sense then in another, looking for something inexpressible between them which would be where to look not only for a possible 'meeting' between Buddhism and the Christian mind, but even for a real spiritual 'symbiosis', at least up to a certain point.

THE 'NON-THEOLOGAL' NATURE OF BUDDHISM AND ITS SPIRITUALITY

The Buddhist refusal to invoke a God and his help, to envisage an association between man and a God who has become 'his God', is something whose meaning goes very deep. What lies behind it, it seems to me, is first and at least implicit criticism of possibly excessive human emphasis in religious behaviour and representations dealing with the Deity. In the second place it is a vigorous attempt by the human spirit to undertake and win the conquest of spiritual liberation using its own resources alone. The way is undoubtedly very hard but it can be found. Here Buddhism rejoins the final passages of Spinoza's *Ethics*.

So there is no need here for a religious faith in order to define one's goal, nor for any necessary divine help in order to reach it. Man can carry out his quest for *nirvana* without this. All he needs is human energy. The core of will in this energy, the autonomy it proves to itself in undertaking the voluntary pursuit of its goal, the power it has to control both from within and in experience, its paths and its final outcome, themselves constitute a criticism and exposure of the religious and theist view of spirituality.

This is not to say that Buddhism sets itself up as a spirituality of man on his own in the sense that this phrase can have in the West, as a sort of 'atheistic humanism', as one can be tempted to say. There are at least two aspects to prevent this: first, the fact of an unbroken solidarity with universal life, a sort of spiritual complicity in the whole world environment, itself exposed to *dukkha* and, as it were, sharing in the human aspiration to liberation; [2] second, the feeling of community amongst those who undertake a similar course of spiritual quest: this is *sangha,* the third refuge for the human being which the Buddhist monk professes to choose together with the Buddha and the Law, which are the first two. Both these considerations are thoroughly human but somehow escape the Western concept of humanism. Buddhism experiences the context of cosmic solidarity more or less completely free from the Western feeling of the superiority and virtual separation of man in his relationship with the whole of the rest of the universe. And what the Buddhist community professes to seek is not man either in the sense of 'the human' of Western humanism, but absolute liberation, the *nirvana* of the spirit—which is something quite different: the other shore that does exist even if 'God' does not, while man and his atheistic humanism are fated to remain on the nearer shore.

Liberation from the native condition of being, access to *nirvana,* the apparent effacing of the empirical individual personality, *anattâ,* as the Buddhism of Theravada calls it: these at first sight seem to belong to a negativity pushed to the metaphysical extreme. The abolition of any desire directed toward actualizations of existence; the onset of this unparalleled experience of 'the farther shore', to which the 'nothingness' of Western mystics and the *Nichts* of Hegelian philosophy seem to be ways of approach. The disillusion finally of the self, the self that alone remains to be sketched out for a little time by the remnants of our bodily condition before physical death. All these things, one might say, are only a spiritual development of the human capability—spiritual in itself—for negative behaviour. It is as though, admittedly beyond the 'no' of direct refusal or of animal violence, or beyond the pathological wounding of the soul, this negative behaviour in its sublimated and well-behaved spirituality were the irreducible autonomous spring, independent of everything else, of the energy inherent in the human being.

Nevertheless, just as *nirvana* is not purely and simply nothing, so the form of Buddhism known as *anattâ* is not purely and simply the material collapse of being. The abolition of desire and the satisfactions it brings, taken to the ultimate limit, becomes peace, a supreme density of peace,[3] and what in the final analysis cannot be called anything other than unlimited contentment, complete happiness if one likes. This is perhaps impossible to explain but it can all be experienced, fulfilled and maintained in the inexplicable act that is life. For those who live by debating with life, it is coming to live that counts. All the rest can be incoherence or silence. Explanations and teaching necessarily become external, with each person remaining responsible for performing them to the extent that he himself succeeds in seeing what he himself has to do.

If one confines one's considerations of Buddhism to these spiritual characteristics, one still, in my opinion, has an unfaithful picture of Buddhism. It is undoubtedly the picture of a very high level of spirituality, capable of producing—as in fact happens—a very pure morality, an extreme courage of will and at the same time—not the least remarkable aspect—an equilibrium in the practice of life which is as sensible as it is simple, on principle detached from every excess, even in a life ardently and persistently vowed to the quest for spiritual liberation. But at the same time, at least for the Christian, this picture is one of a spirituality lacking divine intimacy and the joy of creation, despite so many aspects that seem to resemble Franciscan spirituality. It also lacks St Francis's song of the creatures. It is a spirituality of fascinating but harsh distances, a spirituality of the self-dependence of a force in being that knows no more—or can find no more—than itself and which is determined not to depend on anything but itself. It is a spirituality of stoic or Pelagian parentage we would say in the West. This has led to several forms of criticism more or less current in Western literature, even when the West is looking for ways of drawing closer. These criticisms are at least partly unjust and will not be examined here.

THE 'FRATERNAL' NATURE OF BUDDHISM

Buddhism still possesses something quite different from all we have examined so far. This is something difficult to explain, perhaps particularly so for a Christian. In order to do so he has hardly any resources other than those of his own religion and spirituality. Using these he risks seeming to want to draw a spirituality, a whole complex of human attitudes, into the Christian orbit, when they are what they are for themselves and outside this Christian orbit. This is an attempt at embracing them which I consider unjustified and lacking in sufficient respect for what Buddhism is in itself and bears within itself in its own name. Centred on the quest for *nirvana* or its closer or more distant equivalents according to the diversity of the inner traditions of Buddhism, there are three dispositions of the mind that seem to me basic. Their particular manifestations in practice or in teaching are, in my view, not only witnesses of admirable spiritual values, but also constituents—valid for the whole human race—of subjects for emulation which Christians could often benefit by considering seriously and putting into practice in their own lives. These dispositions are: first, that of the will to be gentle and peaceful; second, that of prayer and the practice of meditation; finally, that of universal goodwill, *maitri,* a goodwill which in the teachings of the *Great Vehicle* should be carried to the point of temporarily renouncing final deliverance so as to help others to start on and follow its course.[4]

These are matters of great significance for the soul and things that, by a strange and scandalous paradox, the ways in which Christianity has been assimilated in the West have threatened to uproot and banish from human existence, particularly Christian existence in these modern times. Nevertheless, it is possible to find an absolutely categorical equivalent in the Gospels for each of these dispositions of the spirit: blessed are the meek, blessed are the peacemakers . . . and again; you must pray all the time . . . and again: love your enemies, do good to those who hate you. St Francis of Assisi used to say of these teachings: 'to the letter, to the letter', indicating the way in which they should be followed. On these absolutely basic points, Buddhist behaviour and preaching show a sort of concordance with the Gospel which, once seen, the Christian must find difficult to resist. So, conversely to what must be said of Buddhism as a spirituality free from any specifically theologal reference, one can emphasize the spiritual similarities existing, as though on principle between the Buddhist attitude and what Christ taught on the spiritual distance to be taken up from the present world with its violence and envies, and on the way in which one should truly become a neighbour to others. On this point, using traditional Christian language which alone appears to be capable of expressing the reality, the Buddhist approach will itself seem to be in a naturally evangelical 'state of grace'. Today this is an even more attractive aspect since, in many cases, modern man is more or less deeply opposed to the idea of the God of religions, while the figure of Jesus continues to appeal to him as an unequalled master, teaching how life among men should be lived.

Many Christians have appreciated this deep resentment and tried to explain it as best they can. A prime example is de Lubac, in the fine first chapter of his *Aspects du bouddhisme* devoted to Buddhist charity,[5] and throughout the whole course of his study of the tradition of *Amidism,* the most popular form of Buddhism.[6] It is not necessary to repeat here what has been said on this subject. The moving picture of human brotherhood and of a sort of immanent 'fraternal grace' balances the feeling of theologal indifference marking the spirituality of *nirvana.* However, it seems to me that our picture of Buddhism would be untrue if it concentrated only on a representation of this fine, high inspiration of human brotherhood, marked by goodwill and freedom from attachment to daily life—particularly if one seeks to make these coincide with a somewhat idealistic picture of Christian charity and one that leaves its specific character largely out of account.

To say without further ado that Buddhist spirituality is non-theologal in nature, while materially true, is a partial betrayal of this spirituality. To say, again without further ado, that its spiritual character has a fine spirit of brotherhood is again a betrayal in another way and perhaps also a betrayal of the Christianity we thereby try to make Buddhism resemble. This is a good illustration of the difficulty I set out at the beginning: attempting to move from the experience of spiritual sympathy to the language that explains it. When one comes to language, reality is as it were to be found in the interface between two positions in the discourse, each distorted by their quest for exactitude. In terms of this intellectual experience there is still one more step to be taken toward a somewhat better understanding of the matter.

CHRISTIAN QUESTIONS AND APPROACHES

Believing in God, trying to live the sort of religious life and Christian experience whose theologal nature I recognize, but with a brotherly interest in the way Buddhism is lived, I find it difficult to imagine that their way has nothing to do with the way I try to live as a Christian. On the contrary, it seems to me that Buddhism shows me a true human spiritual possibility whose characteristics are in some way inscribed in the inner depth of what the Christian can be expected to experience.

Buddhism is a spirituality born of itself outside the cultural threshold of the early genesis of the monotheistic faith of Judaism and before the birth of Christianity itself. These circumstances seem to me an essential consideration; they show how the theologal reference explicitly present at the centre of the monotheistic tradition and on principle ruling the whole theistic and Christic economy of the Christian religion, can be totally lacking from the centre of Buddhism, without making this depart from a truth of the human spiritual condition with regard to its historical formation and the course of its development throughout the progress of humanity. In the religious and spiritual context of India in the sixth century BC, the religious and spiritual experience, both of individuals and of the collective culture of that human quest described by St Paul when he preached to the Athenians (Acts 17:26-28), had reached a stage of complex maturity basically genuine and healthy: this must have been so to make possible the awakening of the Buddha and the beginning of his tradition. Furthermore, believing in God's presence in all creative things and in the life of the Spirit, believing in his providential design for the whole of humanity and for the different configurations of his development throughout his earthly stay, I see nothing impossible in this presence and providence dwelling anonymously, without being in any way recognized (and perhaps without taking the initiative to make himself genuinely recognized), at the heart of the branching-out and flourishing of that part of the whole human spiritual experience represented by Buddhism.

Why not? And why not see this also as a blossoming of what God intended to produce at the heart of creation by his creation of the human creature? Why not again, even though we must consider grace a divine gift to man capable of producing some spiritual transformation of his behaviour, accept that Buddhism can have been visited—as though despite itself—by an authentic evolution of grace in the sense in which Christian theology uses this word? Why cannot *nirvana* itself be a sort of peaceful and silent union with the energy of the divine goodwill, nameless and formless, existing as a withdrawal from all things, but never rejecting anyone who comes toward it? This is what I personally am inclined to think, but without in any way trying to force a similar interpretation on anyone not disposed to understand the fact of Buddhism and its spirituality in this way. Taking the matter from the point of view of a phenomenology of the human fact, Buddhist spirituality seems to me the supremely convincing example of what man can reach existentially, by himself, without a religious faith in the proper sense of the word, without in any case making use of reference to what the word 'God' is taken to signify in the monotheistic religious tradition.

If Buddhism can be seen in this way by a Christian, this would appear to be pregnant with consequence. It in fact provides a privileged attestation to the benefit of theologal religious faith, as though by a sort of prime counter-example of the specificity of this religious faith, which differs from the communalty of beliefs from which no religion is free. There is something original, living and speaking in the monotheistic tradition, embodied in what Jesus himself described as the first commandment of the Law, something that implies the 'second commandment equal to the first' but which is not a simple equivalent to the first, although it is necessary if man is to be able to live his divine sonship happily in Jesus Christ. For the moment there is no need to say more on this point.

This does, however, raise one question—or perhaps two. The first is that of the status of spiritual observance of the 'second command-ment', when the first is not implied or at least entirely overshadowed. The second is that of the status of prayer—or meditation if one prefers—and even more of consecration of life when there is no theologal access to orientate prayer or justify the presence or human experience of the sacred. All this exists at the heart of Buddhism and exists in humanity and for the Christian with his familiar theological and spiritual schemes. It is a great lesson and also poses a great ques-tion to which one should perhaps not wish to provide an over-rapid reply.

It has therefore to be admitted that the actuality of Buddhist experi-ence, the access to what the Buddha had access to, and wished to lead his disciples to, possess—with regard to other beings brought step by step close to the infinite—a virtue similar if not exactly parallel to the theologal experience of the love of God at the heart of the Christian religion truly experienced. The meaning given to behaviour in one and the other, the content of interpretation and of motivations of course differ: the Christian on principle regards his neighbour as a person destined in Jesus Christ to a personal, eternal life just as he considers himself as a personal individual likewise destined to personal, eternal life and even to a body promised to resurrection; Buddhism does not see this 'other' with which existence makes him deal in this way at all, but this makes no difference: there is a broad agreement in the manner of acting. Buddhist compassion for the misery of man in fact holds out a hand to the pity Jesus felt for the crowd harassed by life and scattered like sheep without a shepherd. In both cases the ways of understanding this misery are different but the impulses of pity are the same. This perhaps can teach us all today to grow together in our behaviour before we start debating the different inspiration underlying this behaviour.

So one must admit that without explicitly confessing any God, man is able to pray, meditate, contemplate and lead an existence devoted to something quite other than the profanity of life. The Buddhist experi-ence and the *nirvana* subsisting at its heart are sufficient to indicate—as the *Brahmanic* experience of Hinduism also does though in another way—the difference between the sacred and the whole power of its absolute embodiment. They are sufficient to have given rise to a genuine monasticism with a set of virtues essentially consonant with what Christian tradition has called 'the evangelical counsels': poverty, chastity, abdication of self-will, faithfulness to the law of the commu-nity. They are sufficient to have instituted and organized a way of life entirely directed to what lies beyond life here below, on the farther shore offering sacrifice: precisely what Hinduism calls the essence and true realization of man.

All this must be allowed. All things considered, I think the Christian must find this refreshing to admit, since it shows him—at a time when all human things can be communicated despite their divisions and distribution on this earth—the chance of a true and legitimate spiritual brotherhood, one that goes beyond—though without losing the essential originality of the theologal and Christic order—the imprisonment of the soul in the historical particularity, still existing (and I think destined to last till the end of time), of the Christian line of development within the totality of human experience.

Translated by Paul Burns

Notes

1. Examining the question from the noetic standpoint, it seems to me that what Buddhism expresses by the word *dukkha,* and correlatively, *nirvana,* the spiritual abolition of *dukkha,* is situated on the level of *experience* considered in its most immediately felt and most genuine aspects. *Karma* is an entity corresponding to a certain form of 'human *feeling* for life', a sort of feeling with which an organization of existential experience begins, which can be gone over and which does not provide evidence of itself unless certain conditions are met. *Saṃsāra* implies a *theorization* of existence, based on the experience of *dukkha* and the feeling of *karma*, but involving representations and an interpretation of reality which it is praiseworthy to call into question, and which, in general, the West does not possess. Despite possible communality of experience on the workaday level, progressive differences in feeling, and of theories of existence, make true encounters between the Christian and the Buddhist mind difficult. But careful analysis and sufficient abandonment of naive convictions of exclusive possession by one's own side of true feeling and a right view of existence can turn these very differences into the means of thoughtful encounter, sympathy in depth and mutual respect for the originality of the other's point of view.

2. Suffice here to point out the similarity to what St Paul says of the 'groaning of creation' being like that of the human creature waiting for deliverance from slavery (Rom. 8:20-23).

3. Here again, suffice to mention the possible similarity with what St John says of evangelical peace and the passage in Paul (Phil. 4:7) on the 'peace that passes understanding', the peace that St Benedict wished to see as the motto of his monks.

4. Here again there is a possible correspondence with the inner debate Paul shares with his correspondents in the town of Philippi: 'I want to be gone and be with Christ, which would be very much the better, but for me to stay alive in this body is a more urgent need for your sake. This weighs with me so much that I feel sure I shall survive and stay with you all . . .' (Phil. 1:21-26).

5. H. de Lubac, *Aspects du bouddhisme*, I (Paris, 1951).

6. *Aspects du bouddhisme, II: Amida* (Paris, 1955).

Roger Corless

A Christian Perspective on
Buddhist Liberation

CONFRONTED by a non-Christian, a Christian has tended to convert first and to try to understand later. St Francis Xavier, finding Indian villages full of unbaptized children, put their baptism and instruction before not only his own physical comfort but his spiritual development: 'When I go into those villages, the children do not give me the leisure (*no me dexavan*) to recite my Office, to eat or to sleep, until I have taught them some prayers'.[1]

St Francis was at least working in a nominally Christian region, but some missionaries, notably Protestants, have held that all the unbaptized are destined for hell, and that any other viewpoint debases the Christian message and ends in relativism. The Catholic magisterium has occasionally seemed to take this view, but Pius V, Innocent XI and Clement XI have spoken against it, and the second Vatican Council has come out clearly in favour of 'serving and promoting' the 'spiritual and moral goods' of non-Christian religions.[2] The Council spoke in one guarded sentence about what it considered to be the 'goods' of Buddhism, mentioning the 'radical insufficiency of this changing world' and the 'state of perfect liberation' and the 'highest illumination' attainable either by self-effort or 'help from above'.[3]

In this article I shall look sympathetically at Buddhist liberation in the spirit of the Council and try to find those points on which a Christian could agree fairly readily with a Buddhist, and those points about which a Christian would have serious reservations. I shall attempt to avoid a mere *syllabus errorum*, for the state of mutual understanding between Buddhism and Christianity is still in its infancy and does not yet allow us to be certain that, although we may have different verbal formulations, we necessarily have mutually exclusive intentions. A Christian perspective on Buddhist liberation can at the moment be no more than sketchy and out of focus. Later, perhaps, when Buddhists and Christians understand one another better, a sharper picture may be produced. The present article offers the reader the fruit of more than twenty years' reflection on the subject, but I am prepared to accept that it will eventually prove dated.

Buddhism is clearly a soteriological religion: it states that the human condition is unsatisfactory; it points to a trans-human state which is satisfactory; and it indicates the path from the one to the other. It is what William James called a 'twice-born' religion[4]—the individual must die to himself and be re-born a new creature—and as such it is directly in sympathy with Orthodox and Catholic Christianity, and with most forms of Protestant Christianity. Christian Science is perhaps the only Christian denomination which is clearly non-soteriological and 'once-born' (and in this respect only is closer to Confucianism and Shintoism than to Buddhism), but there is something to be said for Einar Molland's ambiguous classification of this group in what he calls (in *Christendom*, London 1959), 'religious systems containing elements derived from Christianity'.

I shall examine the human condition, salvation and the path in Buddhism, and see how much it seems to accord with Christianity, and, in a concluding section, speak of the Bodhisattva ideal, which is perhaps that which appears most noble in Buddhism from the Christian point of view.

THE HUMAN CONDITION

In his last years, Leonardo da Vinci scribbled again and again in the margins of his notebooks: 'Tell me if anything ever was done?' He drew pictures of storms, calamities and the drowning of everything beneath the mindless waters of primaeval chaos, as if to say: 'All my work, all of anyone's work, is ultimately fruitless, for it perishes'. It is this vision of the souring of things which the Buddhists call *duhkha*, 'unsatisfactoriness', the first of the Four Noble Truths, and which the second Vatican Council called 'the radical insufficiency of this changing world' (*radicalis insufficientia mundi huius*). Everything that is composite (*saṃskṛta*) is impermanent (*anitya*) and will decompose. The Buddhist is surrounded by and partakes in death with a peculiar vividness—the death not only of persons but of things, ideas, and of Buddhism itself, which will eventually decay without trace until it is revived by a new Buddha. It is said that a phenomenon exists for one *kṣaṇa*, a temporal unit assigned various values (such as a sixteenth part of a handclap) but always very small. In the next *kṣaṇa,* another phenomenon appears, similar to and conditioned by but not identical with its predecessor. The Buddhist who has awoken to the First Noble Truth lives always in the Garden of Gethsemane, confronting pain and fighting sleep.

But this alarming condition is, at bottom, nobody's fault. It is caused by selfish desire (*tṛṣṇā*), but this is in turn caused by ignorance (*avidyā*) or, more exactly, by non-gnosis. The unspiritual human is called a *bāla,* a child or simpleton: he does not know what he is doing. A Christian insists that death is a result of sin (Rom. 5:12-4), a free and responsible choice of evil, with full knowledge of the consequences, which then impairs subsequent freedom of choice (*in deterius commutatum*—Council of Orange, D 174). Whether he reads the story of Adam and Eve historically or mythologically, the Christian sees an account of a free choice between a command of God and immediate sensual satisfaction; between cosmic order and personal advantage. A Buddhist *bāla* has not chosen to be a *bāla:* he is morally depraved, but he has not chosen moral depravity. There is no entity against which he has rebelled and which could therefore be wrathful and righteously demand satisfaction. He confesses his transgressions, but not his sins. The Buddha, like Christ, 'cometh down to us in the lowest part of our need', as Julian of Norwich says, but the Buddha does not accuse us of a betrayal of trust. A Christian sinner is more wretched than a Buddhist *bāla* because more perverse, and he cannot be saved merely by the thousand-armed all-merciful Bodhisattva Avalokitésvara; he needs to participate intimately in the destruction and regeneration of the just and merciful Man of sorrows whom he has himself offended.

Buddhists do not offer a linear explanation for the presence of misery. They either dismiss the question as irrelevant, as in the parable of the poisoned arrow (one should remove the arrow, not ask from where it came), or talk of *ādyavidyā,* 'primal ignorance', by which is meant not that there was a time long ago when ignorance began (as, perhaps, there was a time, or a mythological *illud tempus,* when sin began), but that ignorance is the first point of discussion in the conditioned co-arising (*pratītyasamutpāda*) of phenomena. That is, causation (or mutual conditioning, since causation is strictly absent in Buddhism) is represented as a wheel, death causing ignorance causing death. A wheel does not have a point at which it begins, only a point at which one starts to look at it. This lack of a discussion of linear aetiology is of a piece with a lack of a teleology. One is reborn until one gets off the wheel: history goes on until every being gets off the wheel and there is no more history.

It is characteristic of the Semitic monotheisms (Zoroastrianism, Judaism, Christianity and Islám) to claim that every life has meaning, that the universe is a cosmos and not a chaos, that it is coming from and going to somewhere. Martyrs are not just unfortunate, or reaping the fruits of previous misdeeds, they are the seed of the Church. Muslims who die fighting for Alláh go immediately to Paradise. Ahura Mazda will eventually defeat Ahriman. Even the Nazi holocaust must somehow be providentially permitted by Yahweh. And, of course, the crucifixion, apparently the ghastly failure of God's direct intervention, becomes the resurrection.

Buddhists cannot be accused of escapism: the Buddha, it is said, had the opportunity to disappear into *nirvana* directly after his enlightenment but, simply because of compassion (*karuṇā*), he remained to teach for over forty years. Nevertheless, it must seem to a Christian that a Buddhist concentrates on the misery of the phenomenal world only to escape it himself and to help others escape. He does not seem to descend transformatively into the suffering as the Christian can sink into the depths of the desolation of the dying God-Man and make of that very desolation his *Te Deum Laudamus* with the blessed in heaven.

TRANS-HUMAN LIBERATION

Before a Buddhist is finally liberated, he must undergo repeated rebirths in pleasant or unpleasant states as he works out his good and bad *karma*. Rebirth is not a common belief amongst Christians, but it may not be an impossible one. Origen upheld the pre-existence of souls, and his view was never officially condemned.[5] In recent times, a prominent English Methodist, the Rev. Dr Leslie Weatherhead, has argued in favour of rebirth.[6] The Councils of Lyons (1274) and Florence (1439) asserted that souls after death go immediately to heaven, hell or purgatory, and the fourth Lateran Council (1215) condemned the Albigensians, who denied the existence of any purgatory other than re-birth on earth.[7] The focus of attention in all three Councils is on the existence of purgatory, but the magisterium is vague on the *nature* of purgatory and it is silent on rebirth. What in any case seems to give the Fathers trouble is metempsychosis: that is, the successive clothings of an unchanging personal core in changeable bodies. Such a personal core is the Hindu *ātman* (self) and the Jain *jīva* (living-thing). In the West the idea is found in Platonism and Albigensianism.[8] But the Christian doctrines of the unity of the person and the resurrection of the body tolerate no such separable core, and Buddhism also tirelessly denies the existence of an unchanging self-entity under any of the names which Hindus and Jains have given it: 'There is no *ātman* (self), *sattva* (living-being), *jīva* (living-thing) or *pudgala* (personality-substrate), says the Diamond Sutra (section 14). There is, say Buddhists, rebirth, but no permanently identifiable 'thing' which 'is reborn': a difficult doctrine to defend (one simile given is that of a flame passing from candle to candle, and certain schools admit a continuum such as the 'mere "I" ' (*aham-mātra*) which flows from one life to the next) but one on which they maintain the Buddha was quite unequivocal. So a Catholic might be permitted to regard re-birth in the *Buddhist* sense as a disputed question linked with the investigation of whether the doctrine of purgatory might not be incompatible with lives of further purification here or elsewhere.

However this may be, a Buddhist's eventual liberation is a breakthrough from non-gnosis to gnosis. According to Theravāda, he develops at a certain point the wisdom eye (*paññā-cakkhuh*) with which he gazes upon nibbāna. Amongst the Mahāyanists, the Yogācārins teach an enantiomorphic reversal of *vijñāna* (consciousness or mediate knowing) into *jñāna* (wisdom or immediate knowing), at which time the ideas of a thing to be seen (even nirvana) and of a seer to see it, both become meaningless. For the Theravādin, nibbāna is unarisen, and for the Mahāyanist, all things, including nirvana, are observed as in fact unarisen when the faculty known as the Calm Knowledge of Non-Arising (*anutpattikadharmakṣānti*) is obtained. In some sense, then, the achievement of Buddhist liberation is an entry into rest somewhat like the endless sabbaths of Abelard's hymn *O quanta qualia sunt illa sabbata* ('Oh, what are those sabbaths [of the blessed]!'). The precise characteristics of this rest, however, are difficult to assess because it is nearly always described negatively, or more exactly, it is described apophatically; and it is of the nature of apophatic description to preclude, ultimately, all description or non-description.[9] But all is not lost, for the final state is described cataphatically in the so-called Pure Land Sutras.

Although Zen has captured the imagination of the West, Pure Land Buddhism in Japan has twice its number of adherents.[10] It is primarily a religion of faith, and its view of faith in relation to Christianity will be examined in the following section. It derives its name from a belief in the existence of a *jōdo* or 'pure land' (more precisely, 'purified' or 'purifying' land) far beyond the setting sun and ruled over by a powerful and compassionate Buddha called Amita (Amida in Japanese) whose life-span is infinite (*amita*). This land is described in some Sanskrit sutras, but it did not become the object of a special school until about the fifth century AD in China. In Japan the school exists in two major forms, Jōdo Shū ('Pure Land School') and Jōdo Shinshū ('True Pure Land School'), of which the latter, often known simply as 'Shin Buddhism', is the more popular.[11] The description of the Pure Land in the sutras is lavish and baroque: the imagery is that of an ultimate *mela* (Indian fête) in the sky, where everything good is to be found and there is nothing contrary. The commentaries detail the *duḥkha* of this world (and, indeed, of the heavens and the hells) and show how the Pure Land has in every case the appropriate opposite *sukha* ('bliss'), somewhat after the manner of St Anselm of Canterbury's description of heaven as the fulness of joy in *Proslogion, ch. 25.* The pleasures are intensified by a synaesthesia which would have been dear to the heart of Rimbaud. Yet these delights are in no way lascivious. It is regarded as a miracle wrought by the incomprehensible power of Amita that, whereas the senses in this world lead to *rāga* (lust), in the Pure Land they lead to *dharma-prīti* (pious zest). The devotees who here contemplate and invoke Amita will go to him at their deaths (this death is called *ōjō* or 'birth', as a Christian martyr's death is called his *dies natalis,* 'birthday') and, in the Pure Land, gaze in rapt attention upon the beauty of Amita and the reflection of his beauty in each other. The imagery is so close to that of the final cantos of Dante's *Paradiso* that the only element which a Christian misses is the object of the beatific vision: it is not the Triune God, Creator and Lord of the universe, but a Buddha who, although his devotees regard him as the most powerful of Buddhas, and as the creator and sustainer of the Pure Land, is not the sole Buddha, did not create the universe, and cannot in any sense be regarded as a ground of being.[12] The Pure Land differs from the Buddhist heavens, which are numerous temporary lodging-places, by being extra-phenomenal, so that 'birth' there is really 'no-birth', and this is one reason why the Land is called 'pure': it is incomprehensible, unsullied by discursive thought, and fundamentally unarisen. It is called 'The Realm of Non-Arising'.[13] It is therefore a cataphatic description of an apophatic reality. Could the Pseudo-Dionysius have put it any better?

There is, however, a problem of the embodiment or individuality of the blessed in the Pure Land. In art, they are represented as having separate bodies, and the sutras say that all those born there appear as perfect men (not cripples, women or animals), and speak of them in the plural. But the commentaries have them all obtain (or attain to) the *Dharmakāya:* that is, they participate somehow in the one omnipresent and unmanifest Body of Buddha-ness. It is the nature of the *Dharmakāya,* according to the Mahāyānists, to produce (or manifest) *nirmāṇa-kāyas* or Buddhas in human form. Thus, the blessed in the

Pure Land appear in the conditioned realms of *duḥkha* and *saṃsāra* as and when needed and, because the *Dharmakāya* is quite unconditioned, they can so appear instantaneously, and in more than one realm simultaneously. But because the *Dharmakāya* is unconditioned, they do not leave the Pure Land—just as the sun is reflected in rivers and lakes but does not leave the sky.

This super-Einsteinian extra-spatio-temporal activity leaves me in some doubt as to whether it makes sense to speak of 'persons' (in the sense that this word is normally understood in Catholic theology) in the Pure Land at all. Buddhism certainly does not wish to drown everybody in a monistic soup, as a Vedāntin Hindu might, but neither does it wish to have everybody quite separate: it vexingly speaks of 'monistic pluralism' and then, with a smirk, vanishes. Perhaps if we knew what we meant when we say that the saints behold God yet can hear every prayer addressed to them without muddling them, and then can help us on earth while being themselves in heaven, we might be able to evaluate the condition of the blessed in the Pure Land. Maybe we can content ourselves with mulling over the connection between the *vajra-kāya* (indestructible or 'diamond' body), which is the end-product of Tantric Buddhist liberation, and the Pauline description of the resurrected body as a *sōma tēs doxēs* ('glory-body').

THE PATH TO LIBERATION

Buddhism is richly supplied with paths: in this respect, it is closer to Catholicism than to Protestantism, which emphasizes conversion over development. The differences between the paths are very great, but perhaps no greater than those in Christianity, which range from the quiet of a Friends Meeting, through the hubbub of snake-handling groups such as the Dolley Pond Church of God with Signs Following, to the awesome dignity of the divine liturgy of Saint John Chrysostom. The two Buddhist paths with which a Christian feels most immediately at home are those of faith and liturgical contemplation.

(i) The path of faith:

Despite the importance of faith in Christianity, its nature has been relatively little studied,[14] and it has been almost ignored in Buddhism,[15] so that many Westerners are surprised to learn that it plays any part at all in the religion. In fact, it is central to it. As Har Dayal has said, '. . . Gautama Buddha is the centre of the whole movement, and . . . the Doctrine derives its vitality and importance from his personality.'[16] The commonest Buddhist word for faith is *śraddhā* (Pāli, *saddhā*), which is constructed from *śrad*, 'trust', 'assurance', and *dhā*, 'put'. It means to put one's trust in a person considered reliable. It is therefore very close to the definition of St Thomas Aquinas (*Summa Theologica* II-II, q.11, a.1, co.) that faith is assent to someone's words, thus primarily trust in a person and secondarily trust in what is said by that person. This is an elaboration of St. Augustine's view that faith is 'to think while agreeing' (*cum assensione cogitare*—PL 44:963). The anti-intellectual 'leap of faith', which one finds pre-eminently in Søren Kierkegaard, has never been sanctioned by the Catholic magisterium, and in fact the balance between faith and reason was strongly re-asserted by the first Vatican Council (1869-70).

Throughout Buddhism there is an emphasis on faith in the 'Triple Treasure' of the Buddha, his teaching (*dharma*) and his informed community (*saṃgha*). Tibetan Buddhism adds a fourth element, the lama or guru, who unifies the Triple Treasure in himself for his disciple, and to whom holy obedience is due as to a Catholic religious superior. Pure Land Buddhism makes faith in Amita Buddha the principal method of liberation, and at first glance is so close to Christianity that some Jesuit missionaries mistook it for a form of Lutheranism. Karl Barth turns his attention to it as 'the most adequate and comprehensive and illuminating heathen parallel to Christianity',[17] and in a lengthy footnote gives a not altogether accurate description of it and wonders about its significance for the 'true religion' of 'Peniel or Evangelical Reformed Christianity'.

Shin Buddhism distinguishes itself from Zen Buddhism by the *tariki-jiriki* dichotomy. *Jiriki* means 'power of oneself' and *tariki* is 'power of another'. It is this distinction that the Second Vatican Council calls, '. . . perfect liberation . . . by one's own efforts (*propriis conatibus*) or by reliance upon help from above (*superiore auxilio innixi*)'. In Zen, one confronts the sheer cliff of enlightenment and climbs it without footholds by one's own main strength. 'The mosquito bites the iron bull', as the kōan says. Self-help. Or, so it appears. In Shin, one gives up all attempts at gaining enlightenment, and discovers the Name of Amita invoking himself in one's heart. Outside-help. Or, again, so it appears. Since the final awakening is beyond dualism (and beyond monism too) it is not the case that either self-help or outside-help is really operative. But since, cataphatically, one must say something, one uses the *upāya* (means, strategy, or *disciplina arcani*) of *tariki-jiriki*. Before liberation, it *seems* to the *bāla* (child) that either it can use its own powers or it can rely on the power of another. In this connection, the word *superiore* ('from above') in the Council's statement, is rather unfortunate. Amita Buddha is not 'up there', the Pure Land is not a place, it is outside of place and placelessness, Amita is not (as Japanese scholars never tire of saying) the Wholly Other. However, the word *superiore* is not entirely infelicitous. In early Chinese Pure Land Buddhism the Pure Land was at least *pictured* as being many leagues to the West, and the worshipper was urged to perform his devotions here with Amita's aid and then he would be assured of re-birth there in the Pure Land. But once there, all notions of 'birth', 'here and there', 'going and coming', would be given up, the dichotomising intellect engulfed in the non-dual purity of the inner essence of that Realm of Non-Arising.

Then, in thirteenth-century Japan, a remarkable man fired with a vision of simple magnificence, Shinran Shōnin, cried out that the Invocation of Amita Buddha (the *Nembutsu*), which had been regarded as the principal Pure Land praxis,[18] was not something he himself did, but something which was discovered to occur 'by the enabling majesty (*onhakarai*) of the Tathāgata' (*Tannishō*, 'Passages Lamenting Deviations', 11). We should not, as had previously been taught, make a resolution to be re-born in the Pure Land, for it was Amita who had already resolved that we should be so re-born. Faith is not something which the believer stirs up in himself for Amita, but something which Amita has for the believer. And the moment of this discovery, said his disciple Kakunyo, is 'the end of the world' for the believer (*Shūjishō*, 'Passages on Perseverance', 5): it is a sort of realised eschatology.

From all of this it may seem that a Catholic, at least (but not a Barthian?), finds himself closer to early Pure Land Buddhism, where there is a synergy between the faith of the human and the power of the Buddha (even though Amita is certainly not God nor is the Pure Land Heaven), than with Shin Buddhism, where everything collapses into an all-competent Other Power which, in effect if not in theory, appears pantheistic. This synergy is even more evident in what follows.

(ii) The path of liturgical contemplation:

Whereas Theravādins offer worship (*pūjā*) to the deities and to the Buddha, but do not regard this as of direct assistance to liberation, and the Zen School attacks the devoidness (*śūnyatā*) of things with minimal liturgical support, Tantric Buddhism makes symbol and ceremony one of the chief vehicles to enlightenment. Tantric Buddhism, which is an element in most forms of Tibetan Buddhism, and is found in Japan as the Shingon Shū or Mantra School, is based on a series of texts called tantras, whereas all other forms of Buddhism are based on texts called sutras. Sutras are open to inspection by all, but Tantras may be investigated only after proper preparation. The language of a Tantra may be symbolic, in which case it is unintelligible without special instruction, or it may be perfectly comprehensible but contain some teachings (such as the use of sexual desire in a manner calculated to liberate the practitioner from sexual desire) which could be dangerously misinterpreted if made generally available. The ritual based on the tantras may also be either symbolic or comprehensible but not openly transmitted. In any case the distinctive characteristic of tantric Buddhism is something called 'the mystery' (Japanese, *mitsu*), that is, something whose innerness is unavailable to the ordinary practitioner. St Augustine's famous definition of a sacrament as an outward and visible sign of an inward and spiritual grace also serves quite well as a definition of a tantric 'mystery', and indeed *sacramentum* is, in the early Church, the Latin translation of the Greek word *mysterion*.

The tantric mysteries are certain acts of the person. As in Catholicism, the acts are threefold: of the body, of the speech and of the mind. The bodily acts are called *mudrās* (hand gestures), the vocal are *mantras* (sounds, sometimes intelligible and sometimes not, frequently ejaculatory invocations), and the mental actions are called *smṛtis* (contemplative recollections or intentions). Ritual implements and musical instruments may be used. A tantric liturgy is a series of linked but discrete acts each composed of a specific *mudrā* united with its appropriate *mantra* and *smṛti*. When performed properly, they become sacraments of liberation which in some sense are effective *ex opere operato:* that is, they are in and of themselves a source of grace (*adhiṣṭhana,* 'support') and power (*prabhava*). Many tantric liturgies are performed publicly and it is regarded as liberating to observe them even without understanding their meaning. Their full effect, however, occurs only when their significance is consciously appropriated: the Japanese call this *sammitsu kaji,* 'the synergy of the Three Mysteries': that is, the Buddha 'adds' (*ka*) his power and the disciple 'holds' (*ji*) onto it in the three (*san*) mysteries (*mitsu*). Reading an account of the 'Life Prolonging Ceremony' (*tse'-grub*), a Tibetan liturgy in which bread (*torma*) and wine (or rice-beer) are consumed, one almost feels as though one had happened upon an eastern variant of St Thomas Aquinas' discussion of the mass. When one sees the high lamas in full vestments, which include something strikingly akin to a Catholic cope and mitre, hears their antiphonal chanting and observes their rosaries, images, incense and holy water, one can easily sympathize with the thirteenth-century Franciscan visitors to the Great Khan, who thought they had at long last found Prester John, the mythical Christian priest-king of the East.

But though a Catholic may feel very much at home in the midst of all this, he is liable to be overwhelmed by the very richness and variety of it. There seems to be a different ceremony or empowerment (*wang,* something like an ordination) for every conceivable stage on the Path.

The Epistle to the Hebrews claims that the multiplicity of the Jewish sacrifices is a mark of their effectiveness being no more than partial. The one sacrifice of Christ, however, from which all the Catholic sacraments draw their life, is perfect and sufficient (see especially Heb. 10). A Catholic theologian should find much to stimulate his own understanding of rites and sacraments in tantric Buddhism, but he must suggest that it is in the crucified and risen Christ that they find their fulfilment.

THE BODHISATTVA IDEAL

In the Theravādin texts, the Buddha is called the Bodhisatta until the moment of his enlightenment. Only thereafter is he Buddha ('awakened'). Mahāyāna raises the condition of the Bodhisatta (Sanskrit, *Bodhisattva*), the state of becoming-a-Buddha, to its highest ideal, and recommends it for everyone. A Mahāyāna Bodhisattva is someone whose present or future spiritual development is sufficient to allow him to become a Buddha, enter *nirvana* and leave the phenomenal world, but out of compassion he decides not to leave, resolving to remain in *saṃsāra* suffering alongside deluded beings until all of them shall have entered *nirvana* ahead of him. He puts himself at the disposal of beings, human and non-human, even at the risk of his own life. There are many stories of Bodhisattvas having given their limbs or their whole bodies for the sake of others. Sometimes this occurs literally, as in the cases of self-immolation recently performed in Viet-Nam, but more often the practice is spiritualized. Being asked for his body, says the *Śikṣāsamuccaya* ('Compendium of Spiritual Exercises') ch. 1, the Bodhisattva spends himself in the service of others; asked for his tongue, he speaks a kind word, and so on.

A Christian immediately thinks of Jesus' commands concerning selfless love (for instance, Mt. 6:27-36) which culminated in his own crucifixion. Again, Buddhists sometimes refer to Jesus as a great Bodhisattva. The ideal is beautifully expressed by the modern Japanese poet Kenji Miyazawa, in lines he wrote while seriously ill. The poem is now one of the most popular in Japan, and appears on samplers and wall-hangings:

> Bending neither to the rain
> Nor to the wind
> Nor to snow nor to summer heat,
> Firm in body, yet
> Without greed, without anger,
> Always smiling serenely.

Eating his four cups of rough rice a day
With bean paste and a few vegetables,
Never taking himself into account
But seeing and hearing everything,
Understanding
And never forgetting.
In the shade of a pine grove
He lives in a tiny thatched hut: ·
If there is a sick child in the east
He goes and tends him:
If there is a tired mother in the west
He goes and shoulders her rice sheaves:
If there is a man dying in the south
He goes and soothes his fears:
If there are quarrels and litigation in the north
He tells them, 'Stop your pettiness'.
In drought he sheds tears,
In cold summer he walks through tears.
Everyone calls him a fool.
Neither praised
Nor taken to heart.

That man
Is what I wish to be.[19]

This isolated cry of a present-day Bodhisattva seems to a Christian like a jewelled stone that asks to be picked up and set in the mosaic below Jesus Pantocrator in the basilica of the *Heilsgeschichte*, on salvation-history, where it might shine with a more significant lustre. But for a Buddhist it no doubt already has its place in the mystery of the Dharmadhātu.

Notes

1. *Epistolae Sancti Francisci Xaverii aliaque eius scripta,* ed. G. Schurhammer, SI, & I. Wicki, SI (Rome, 1944), Vol. I, p. 148, lines 21-23.

2. 'Excursus: The Omnipresence of Grace', *Commentary on the Documents of Vatican II* (New York & London), vol. III, pp. 90-93; *Conciliorum Oecumenicorum Decreta* (Bologna, third ed., 1973), p. 969, lines 28-31.

3. *Conciliorum Oecumenicorum Decreta,* p. 969, lines 11-16.

4. William James, *The Varieties of Religious Experience* (London, 1902), p. 166.

5. The so-called Origen anathemas were attached to the text of the second Council of Constantinople (533), and W. Y. Evans-Wentz, *Tibet's Great Yogi Milarepa* (Oxford, 2nd ed., 1951), p. 11, n. 3, cites the anathema against psychic pre-existence as definitive for what he calls 'the church-council Christian'. But these anathemas have been shown not to be authentic. *Conciliorum Oecumenicorum Decreta* (op. cit.), p. 106.

6. Leslie D. Weatherhead, *The Case for Re-Incarnation* (Tadworth, Surrey, 1957). See also Quincy Howe, Jr., *Reincarnation for the Christian* (Philadelphia, 1974).

7. A Mrs Smith, an English housewife, while undergoing psychiatric treatment, has given an account of what she claims to be her former life as an Albigensian in the French Midi. The most diverting aspect of her case is the series of ballads in the Langue d'Oc dialect which she wrote as an English schoolgirl with only a passing knowledge of standard French. Cf., Arthur Guirdham, *The Cathars and Reincarnation* (London, 1970).

8. There are so many similarities between Albigensianism and Jainism that one suspects some form of diffusion of Jain ideas through the Bogomils into Albigensianism: for instance, both Jains and Albigensians radically oppose matter to spirit, and distinguish socially between celibates who are bound by severe ascetical rules and general believers who have few regulations; and both admire the practice of voluntarily fasting to death. When the Greeks talked of the Indian *gymnosophoi* (naked wise ones) they may have been referring to the Digaṃbara (sky-clad) branch of Jainism.

9. For a discussion of Eastern and Western apophatic mysticism, see H. Dumoulin, *Östliche Meditation und christliche Mystik* (Freiburg & Munich, 1966), pp. 98-126.

10. Zen, 10,150,010 adherents; Pure Land, 20,941,532 adherents. Figures as of 31 December 1970. *Japanese Religion, A Survey by the Agency for Cultural Affairs* (Tokyo & Palo Alto, 1972), p. 239.

11. Studies of Shin Buddhism are numerous in Japanese but very rare in Western languages. D. T. Suzuki, *Shin Buddhism* (New York, 1970) is a readable short introduction. Alfred Bloom, *Shinran's Gospel of Pure Grace* (Association for Asian Studies Monographs, Tucson, 1965), gives a competent overview of the school. An important collection of texts has been translated by Hans Haas, *Amida Buddha unsere Zuflucht* (Quellen der Religions-Geschichte, Vol. 2) (Göttingen, 1910). For early Pure Land Buddhism, see my dissertation, *T'an-luan's Commentary on the Pure Land Discourse* (University of Wisconsin Ph.D., 1973).

12. See my article, 'Monotheistic Elements in Early Pure Land Buddhism', *Religion*, 6:2 (Autumn, 1976), pp. 176-89.

13. In Chinese there is a pun on the 'birth' of a being and the 'arising' of an event, both of which are rendered by the character *shêng*.

14. A good historical study is James A. Mohler, SJ, *Dimensions of Faith Yesterday and Today* (Chicago, 1969).

15. The only worthwhile discussion would seem to be that of Kōtatsu Fujita, *Genshi Jōdo Shisō na Kenkyū* (A Study of Early Pure Land Thought) (Tokyo, 1970), pp. 586-603.

16. Har Dayal, *The Bodhisattva Doctrine in Buddhist Sanskrit Literature* (London, 1932), p. 32.

17. Karl Barth, *Church Dogmatics*, Vol. I part 2, trans. G. T. Thomson & Harold Knight (Edinburgh & New York, 1956), p. 340 (*Die kirchliche Dogmatik*, I:2, Zürich, 1945, p. 372). For a Shin Buddhist reply, see Katsumi Takizawa, 'Jōdo Shinshū to Kirisutokyō: Kāru Baruto no Kyakuchū ni yosete' (Shin Buddhism and Christianity considered in relation to Karl Barth's Footnote), in *Jōdo Shinshū to Kirisutokyō* (Shin Buddhism and Christianity), ed. Mitsuyuki Ishida & Katsumi Takizawa (Kyoto, 1974), pp. 377-443.

18. The Nembutsu exhibits many similarities to the Orthodox 'Jesus Prayer'. See Ernst Benz, 'Nembutsu und Herzensgebet', in *Buddhism and Culture/Bukkyō to Monka*, ed. Susumu Yamaguchi (Kyoto, 1960), pp. 126-49. For a wider study of repetitive devotional mantra (and its instrument the rosary) in general, see my article, 'The Garland of Love: A History of Religions Hermeneutic of Nembutsu Theory and Practice' in *Essays in Buddhism*, ed. A. K. Narain (in press).

19. 'November Third', in *The Penguin Book of Japanese Verse*, trans. Geoffrey Bownas & Anthony Thwaite (Harmondsworth, 1964), pp. 201-2.

Mervyn Fernando

The Buddhist Challenge to Christianity

PREAMBLE

THIS reflection contains a personal element which I think needs no
apology. The purpose of this essay is to show how an encounter with
Buddhism in a Buddhist country can affect one's Christian belief and
practice. It is a personal intellectual reflection rather than an academic
study.

Western readers may tend to think that living in a Buddhist country
automatically implies an encounter with Buddhism. This is certainly
not true of the average Christian, if we take encounter as meaning
challenge to, and dialogue with, another world-view. Undoubtedly a
Christian is more or less influenced by certain Buddhist attitudes and
values, according to his degree of Christian formation (or lack of it) and
proximity to a Buddhist milieu.[1] My Christian upbringing in a Catholic
home, education in Catholic schools, and later studies at a seminary
isolated me effectively from any experience of encounter with the
Buddhism of my national milieu. Buddhism was represented to me in
its external manifestations of *Wesak* (birth-day of the Buddha) celebra-
tions with colourful lights and lanterns, *pirita* (chanting), *poya* (full-
moon day) *puja* (offerings), *bana* (discourse by a monk in a temple),
processions with elephants and dancers, and the like—all of which
really bear counter-witness to the Buddhism I encountered later. My
experience would be typical of the average Christian reared in a Christian home and school. The ghetto existence of the Catholic institution
which prevailed then, and by-and-large still does so, effectively insu-
lated us from contact with the heart and soul of Buddhism. Since
Christian community is a small minority, this is sociologically and pas-
torally understandable. It is still necessary to make a conscious and
deliberate effort to break the bond and to encounter Buddhism in Sri
Lanka, which prides itself on being the Dhammadipa, the Island of
(Buddhist) Righteousness.

Encounter with Buddhism is not without serious problems. From a Christian it demands a deep understanding of, and commitment to, his own faith, and an openness to an entirely different world-view expressed in a different set of categories. In Sri Lanka there is the added problem of a still lingering suspicion on the part of Buddhists about the *bona fides* of the Christian overture of dialogue. I have often been frustrated by the implicit or explicit defensive attitudes of even learned and eminent Buddhists in our dialogue groups. The reaction (or over-reaction) to Christian domination of the island by western (Christian) colonial *régimes*[2] has still not died out though it is much less strong than in the nineteen-fifties, soon after political independence.

Finally, the Buddhism I have encountered is the Theravada Buddhism of Sri Lanka which has flourished here as the majority religion of the country for over two-thousand years. Sri Lanka claims, with good reason, to be the centre of Theravada Buddhism in the world.

CHALLENGE TO CHRISTIANITY

The most significant result of an encounter with Buddhism as a whole is to reveal the possibility and fact of a dialectically opposite vision of the human predicament together with an answer to it. It is as if one suddenly realized that the figure of the cup in the picture could also be seen as two faces looking at each other.[3] It may be objected that the analogy could be applied even to two different philosophies: for example, classical Greek and modern existential philosophy. But there is a difference. Buddhism, contrary to some misconceptions among Christians, does not offer itself only as a philosophy or system of thought, but as a way of total human liberation, or in Christian terms, of salvation. It is both theory and praxis. It shows man the way to go from a condition analyzed as relative, impermanent and unsatisfactory, *dukka*,[4] to the unconditioned Absolute of *Nirvana*. It is therefore like Christianity a religion, embracing anthropology, a cosmology, a soteriology and an eschatology. Buddhism is perhaps the highest expression of a comprehensive non-revealed religion.

Let us examine some of the specific features of the dialectical alternative that Buddhism posits *vis-à-vis* Christianity.

Firstly, it is non-revealed: that is, solely elaborated by a rational analysis of human nature and experience in history. This analysis is not just philosophical; it is more psychological—a deeply perceptive laying-bare of human experience and the consequences thereof. The Buddha did not do this as intellectual exercise for its own sake. The *raison d'être* was liberation, *vimukthi*, just as the analysis of a patient's symptoms by a doctor is directed to the remedy or deliverance from the sickness. The remedy naturally 'fits' or negates the disease—they hold together. In the Buddha's analysis, deliverance or *vimukthi* from the disease of *dukkha* lies in the cessation of *karma* in enlightenment or *Nirvana,* which can be achieved by the practice of the Noble Eightfold Path.[5] On the other hand, the specific feature of Christianity is that it is a revealed religion: that is, its basic insights into the historical human condition, the goal of liberation or salvation, as well as the path to it, are all given by a divine revelation. It is not of human origin. Only the deductions and consequences of these basic revealed truths have been elaborated and systematized by human reason in Christian theology.

Secondly, in Buddhism a man must liberate himself by his own effort. The Buddha is not the saviour. He is only teacher, guide and model. 'Therefore, Ananda, be an island unto yourself, a refuge unto yourself, seeking no external refuge; with the teaching as your island, the teaching your refuge, seeking no other refuge'.[6] The Buddha does not demand faith in himself. Even his teaching must be examined and accepted on the conviction of the disciple. But Christianity, being a revealed religion, necessarily demands faith—faith in the God who reveals and manifests himself. God's revealed word must be accepted unquestioningly in faith. This faith itself is a grace, an unmerited gift given by God to man. In other words man can do nothing to save himself; salvation comes to him as a gift through the unique divine saviour Jesus Christ.

Thirdly, Buddhism is atheistic. This is undoubtedly the most shocking aspect of Buddhism for the Christian. Buddhism does not admit the notion of a personal God, a God who creates, redeems and loves. But it does posit something transcendent: *Nirvana,* which is the Unconditioned. This is also the final end of man, the goal of his self-liberating effort. *Nirvana* transcends all conditioned (created) reality; it is beyond all definition and description. The Buddha remained silent on questions about Brahman (God) and the origin of the world.[7] In contrast, in Christianity, Christ is the expression and manifestation of the transcendent, omnipotent God, who is man's creator and final end. He has shown himself to man in a personal way in Jesus Christ: 'He who has seen me has seen the Father'.[8] Jesus is also man's redeemer and the way back to the Father. The heart and soul of Christianity is God and his self-revelation in Jesus Christ inviting man's redemptive response.

I have always found the comprehensive sweep and rigorous consistency of the Buddhist analysis of the human condition very impressive. The Buddha is without doubt one of the world's seers, thinkers and mystics—a truly Enlightened One. Starting from an empirically-established fact of human experience, Buddhism elaborates a rationally consistent and sophisticated structure of cause-effect relationships regarding that experience and liberation from it.[9] Connected concepts about the self, action, death, purification and so on are in harmony with the main structure. They cannot, in fact, be correctly understood outside that conceptual framework. Some Christian thinkers have often succumbed to the temptation of isolating individual concepts in Buddhism and comparing them with corresponding concepts in Christianity. The result is often distortion and misunderstanding. A good example of this is the criticism of the notions of *anatta* and transmigration by the Christian concept of soul, which belongs to another conceptual framework.[10] This, however, does not prevent us from making use of the *insights* given by a particular concept in Buddhism in order to examine a corresponding or similar concept in the Christian faith with very fruitful results.[11]

FAITH AND REASON

Buddhism claims to be a religion of reason, to be accepted critically as such and not on the authority of someone else, not even of the Buddha. Buddhism therefore does not need an apologetics to establish its reasonableness. It even invites its own rejection. The secular man of the modern world could not ask for anything more congenial. But the price of that rejection is prolongation of the *dukkha* condition in *samsara*. The individual is free to choose—with responsibility for consequences of the choice. The way of liberation is however a way of hard work and renunciation, of detachment—a very unpalatable proposition for a modern man. The choice of the way involves an element of faith—faith in the experience of the Buddha as normative for liberation. The neophyte in effect accepts, on the word of the Buddha, that on following the path indicated and taken by him, he will also reach the same goal of Enlightenment and *Nirvana*. At the outset the neophyte will not see for himself that it is so, but he has reason to be confident. This is akin to the experience of reasonable confidence in common-life situations. If I am looking for the road from Colombo to Kandy and I am shown that road by one who has already used it, I will naturally take his word unless I suspect that he intends to deceive me. Belief or confidence is directed not so much to the person as to a course of action which seems reasonable and has produced results already. The thrust of the Buddha's teaching is that the follower should see for himself the truth of the path as he goes along. Plenty of allowance is made for the gradual development of insight with time and effort throughout a man's life-cycle, or even through several cycles.

As a revealed religion, Christianity must demand faith in the revealing person, on the basis of his credentials. Everything hangs on: 'You are the Christ, the Son of the living God'.[12] But unless this 'blind' belief (at the beginning) is progressively turned into a 'seeing' through encounter with the person of Jesus Christ, it will have to be maintained by a strenuous act of the will. This is what many Christians are called upon to do. But with the growing strength of secularization and humanism, that act of the will is strained beyond endurance. Hence the modern crisis of faith. If the Church had been more Buddhistic in its catechesis, if it had fostered and encouraged the faithful to see and experience the way, the truth and the life for themselves, instead of insisting on an unenlightened acceptance of doctrines on the sheer authority of the Church, this crisis might not have occurred. To add to the problem, the faithful have been made to bear a heavy burden of undigested doctrine under the cover of faith. The important distinction between faith in Jesus Christ and theology or doctrinal formulations in Denzinger, the Manuals and Catechisms, has been neglected. The Christian come of age in a secular world is throwing the baby out with the bath-water. Little wonder that the de-Christianized 'Christian' is attracted to the various forms of rational and experiential Buddhism.

SELF-LIBERATION AND GOD-LIBERATION

The Buddhist position that man must liberate himself is the antithesis of the Christian one that all salvation is from God. Again, as stated earlier, these positions must be placed and understood in their proper contexts. But the insight of Buddhism about the need for personal striving and responsibility in the salvific task is illuminating. The Church, seen mostly as institution, has been for the faithful the dispenser of grace and salvation. The faithful merely fulfilled the conditions required. In the sacramental action itself the essential thing was the correct performance of the rite—a strict adherence to matter and form. Then the effect operated by itself, *ex opere operato*. The conscious, intelligent and active engagement of either the minister or the recipient was not given great importance. This ritualistic dispensation of salvation in the Church was not very different from the Brahministic ritualism which the Buddha condemned and rejected in his lifetime. Instead he put the full responsibility on man himself. It was man's understanding, intention and action which mattered. There was no need of mediation of any kind. Each one is his own refuge.

Today we see among Christians a movement of liberation from the tutelage of the Church, a reaction against a *régime* of restrictive protection and control by laws, rules and regulations. The Christian is struggling for the independence and responsibility which he feels have been denied him. He no longer wants to be a minor. Many have dropped out, opting for a non-institutional Christianity, which will give priority to responsible self-determination (self-liberation?) according to one's conscience, awareness and freedom.

The Buddhist experience also shows that religion and religious practice can be maintained with minimal structure and authority. Though Buddhism in Sri Lanka is much less organized centrally and hierarchically than Christianity there is a remarkable homogeneity of belief and practice in essential matters. They have become part and parcel of the way of life of the people. Not only Buddhism but all Eastern religions in general have subordinated doctrine to life, *logos* to *pneuma,* structure to movement. The letter kills but the spirit quickens.

The Buddhist feels obliged to be moral—to be right in thought, word and action—not because of an extrinsic motivation of law, or of divine reward or punishment, but of the intrinsic motivation of self-development or self-liberation. Buddhism dispels the Christian fear that unless there is a binding law connected with sanctions of a supernatural order the moral law cannot be maintained. Certainly the realization of the moral order is fallible and imperfect, just as sin is a reality in the Church. But it is accepted in principle, and within human limitations, in practice too.

GOD AND ATHEISM

Paradoxically, it is the so-called atheism of Buddhism (or, more correctly, its silence about God or the Absolute) that could make the most significant contribution to our understanding of the God of faith. In many ways the silence of the Buddha is an effective antidote to much profitless God-talk in Christianity. Firstly, the Buddha teaches us that silence is the *only possible* 'talk' about God because he is unnamable and unthinkable. Every name or concept we predicate about God is a blasphemy—it makes him less than God. Even the most universal concept of being does not help because it too arises from our finite minds and experience of finite reality. The traditional defence of theology that predication about God is analogical would not escape this criticism. It would be seen by the Buddha as a vain and invalid subterfuge, a refusal to go the whole hog. He would suspect that our untiring efforts to conceptualize God are unconsciously motivated by a need to posit a transcendent, and therefore an unshakeable, crutch for our insecurity and anxiety.

The Buddha would go even further and say that the question itself is meaningless, a non-question not subjectively but objectively. In other words the silence of the Buddha is not an answer to the question, on par with answers given before him by others. By his silence he challenges the questioner to look at the question and by implication to look at himself. The very asking of the question implies that the questioner has some concept of God, otherwise he could not ask the question. Every question presupposes the conditions of intelligibility of the answer too. If the unthinkable has already been thought of, the question has become a contradiction. If the Absolute is questionable it is no longer absolute. No question can even be posed about the Absolute.[13]

The Buddha relentlessly pushes man to accept his human limitations and radical contingency without reserve. The worst form of *karma*-generating *tanha* (desire) could be the *tanha* of the Absolute. By destroying the God-seeking question the Buddha has also catharsized the ego of the questioner.

It seems to me that this line of thinking pushes out the very limits of natural theology (theodicy) consistently and daringly. The Buddha was able to do so because he did not have the help or the 'obstacle' of revelation. Christian natural theology, or what it is supposed to be, is a disguised faith-theology. St Thomas' proofs of the existence of God are helpful to the believer. As purely logical arguments they present formidable difficulties.[14] The Buddha recognizes very rightly that conviction about, and acceptance of, the Absolute will come only through experience and encounter, and not by rational argumentation. Hence his unremitting preoccupation with orthopractice rather than with orthodoxy. Practice not speculation will result in experience and encounter. Get on the way and the rest will follow.

The Church has always been very pre-occupied with orthodoxy—definitions of dogma, heresy and even the persecution of heretics. An enormous amount of time and energy has been expended to these ends. All the general councils of the Church except the last concerned themselves at least partly with dogmatic definitions and anathemas. Volumes have been written by way of exposition, explanation and comment on dogmatic definitions. The Buddha's whimsical question about all this would be, how much have these speculations about God brought the faithful to a liberating experience with him? Or have they distracted them from that experience. The more one talks about God the more he eludes one's grasp. In the eastern religious traditions, it would be meaningless to talk about God without having experienced him. But the one who has experienced the Absolute will not talk about it, because—like the Buddha—he cannot.

We recognize here the mystical-contemplative aspect of encounter with the Absolute, which is really the only one. In fact, after the Buddha and the *dhamma,* the third 'gem' of Buddhism is the *sangha* (monkhood), which exemplifies the practice of the Noble Eightfold Path, in detachment from the world, moral effort and meditation. It is practically impossible for a lay person in the world to attain *arhatship* (sainthood). The mystical-contemplative tradition of Christianity which could meet Eastern religions more sympathetically has not been given priority in the mission Churches of the East. Attempts have been made however during the last few years, especially in India, to present the contemplative face of Christianity to the East.

SUMMARY AND CONCLUSION

A deep Encounter with Buddhism jolts a thoughtful Christian out of the smug complacency of an apparently unshakeable, all-embracing world-view. When parallels and comparisons can be drawn with other religions, for example, with Islam and even Hinduism, Buddhism confronts Christianity with its antithesis. Three of these antithetical points were considered above: no God, no Faith and no God-salvation. If (with Vatican II) we accept that God is at work in other religious traditions,[15] Buddhism presents the startling fact of his self-revelation in self-negation. This antithetical experience about God and the world, about the All, is most disturbing and most rewarding for the human soul.

Notes

1. For example, Buddhist and Hindu beliefs and practices regarding evil spirits (demons of all kinds) and their human manipulation by means of charms, talismans and sacrificial rites are prevalent among Christians.

2. The Portuguese and the Dutch occupied and ruled parts of the country, successively, for three hundred years, introducing Catholicism then Protestantism. The British ousted the Dutch and succeeded in annexing the whole country at the beginning of the nineteenth century. They granted independence to Sri Lanka (then Ceylon) in 1948.

3. A figure often found in psychology books, in which the space between two facing profiles is seen as a cup or chalice.

4. I assume the reader's familiarity with the central concepts of Buddhism such as *dukkha, karma, samsara, tanha, Nirvana*. These are explained in any standard text on Buddhism. See, for instance, Walpola Rahula, *What the Buddha Taught* (New York, 1962).

5. The Noble Eightfold Path (the fourth Noble Truth) is so called because it consists of eight steps or categories: right understanding, right thought, right speech, right action, right livelihood, right effort, right mindfulness, and right concentration.

6. Digha Nikaya XVI (Maha-Parinibbana Sutta), 2,33. English text from, *Last Days of the Buddha* (Kandy, Sri Lanka, 1974), p. 28.

7. Cf. Majjima-Nikaya, Cula-Malunkya-Sutta, 63.

8. John 14:9.

9. The conditionality and interdependence of existential factors operating in human life (and all life) are explained in the formula of conditioned Genesis, *Paticca-Samupadda*.

10. I have elaborated on this problem in 'Self, Reality and Salvation in Buddhism and Christianity' in *Int. Phil. Quarterly*, Vol. XII, 3 (September 1972), pp. 415-25.

11. A good, recently-published example is Lynn A. de Silva, *The Problem of the Self in Buddhism and Christianity* (Study Centre for Religion and Society, Colombo, Sri Lanka, n.d.).

12. Mt. 16:16.

13. Raymond Panikkar calls this the silence of the question. Cf., 'Nirvana and the Awareness of the Absolute' in *The God Experience*, ed., Joseph P. Whelan (New York, 1971), pp. 81-99.

14. Some recent studies of these difficulties are: Plantinga Alwin, *God, Freedom and Evil* (London, 1975); Charlesworth, M. J., *The Problem of Religious Language* (Englewood Cliffs, 1974).

15. *Declaration on the Relationship of the Church to Non-Christian Religions, 2.*

PART III

Bulletins

Michael Rodrigo

Buddhist-Christian Dialogue in Sri Lanka

INTRODUCTION

RUDYARD Kipling, child of the West, met the East at the doorstep of
eastern culture with a strange allusion to the encounter: 'O East is East
and West is West and never the twain shall meet'. No one did more for
the twain to meet than Pope John XXIII and the second Vatican Council. The sigh and the song meant symbols of hope resurgent when he
sighed for wayward ways of the past and sang of hope in the future.
The Council he launched found a world climate ready for dialogue, for
of the 2312 Fathers at the final vote on the Declaration on Other Religions (or Non-Christian Religions) 2221 voted for it, and 88 said 'no' to
the document with two voting *juxta modum*.

Sri Lanka ('the sacred, resplendent isle'), a pear-shaped pendant of
the sub-continent of India, termed Ceylon in recent times, and earlier
Serendib, Taprobane, Celiao and Zeilan by different people at different
times, received the Buddhist doctrine under King Devanampiyatissa.
To the animist it was good news that morality for self and others was
more meritorious than worship of stick or stone, and more endowed
with meaning than appeasement of a tree-god. Buddhism in its
Theravāda form came to stay as a companion of the court, paramour of
princes and people, dear to dynasties as it moved down Lanka's history at its own pace, now gathering momentum, now 'stagnant' as an
acquisition, or again needing a booster-shot in the shape of a reform of
its institutions, and in more recent years, challenging Christianity's
right to existence in an era of naïve nationalistic sentiment a few years
after the second World War when nationalism seemed to be a desperate
remedy for most of the ills of South Asia.

Sri Lanka, basically religious, has four strands of religion woven into its national life: Hinduism, which may have been here before the Christian era in a primitive form; Islam from after the tenth century in the wake of Arabian trade; Buddhism; and Christianity. There is even mention of a group of Nestorian Christians in the north-central area early in the first millennium after Christ. Today's Buddhist-Christian dialogue reckons more with multilateral than with bilateral dialogue, but for purposes of my study I shall restrict myself to a possible deepening of relationships between Buddhism and Christianity. Official Christianity came in three waves with mixed intentions: this-worldly ambition and other-worldly ardour, food and faith, spices and sacraments so that the men who brought Christianity were soldiers and missionaries at first, then 'ousters' and finally 'colonizers', in three invasions: the Roman Catholic Portuguese in 1505, the Reformed Dutch in 1656, and the Anglican English in 1796.

Men of their times, the Portuguese *lascarins* were helped by their veneer of Christianity to raze to the ground much that the local people held sacred in edifice and custom. The Dutch, not to be outdone in a generous mixing of motives of military might and raw reform, persecuted Catholic Christians, while the Anglicans concentrated on a subtle persecution of the peasantry and an invitation to foreign workers. Memories die hard. The Buddhist collective unconscious remembers this unforgettable experience.[1] Years of reconciliation and healing are needed. The hitherto numbers-bound, conversion-prone Christian is to be a reconciler today. The tide turned at Vatican II.

DIALOGUE BEFORE AND AFTER VATICAN II

The priestly minister is often at the frontier of orthodoxy and orthopractice: this was so in October 1964, when a probe was launched among 160 priests to find out the opportuneness of Buddhist-Christian dialogue. Questions ranged from the feasibility of a priests' seminar, to the attitudes of people to dialogue.[2] The positive answers revealed a trend among priests since 1959 to see in Buddhism, 'the radical insufficiency of this shifting world'.[3] This trend matured after the conciliar declaration, since the same Spirit of the Word is Spirit of the Word made flesh, the risen Christ. The pace-setting of Vatican II thus found an echo, especially after the courses at the National Catholic Seminary in Kandy where priests have been trained *in* and *for* Sri Lanka since 1955. Fr Wilhelm Hendriks, OMI, has conducted a theology course with a Hindu and Buddhist background since 1955. Mellawaratchi, a former Buddhist monk of fifteen years' standing gave a course in Notional Buddhism for two semesters in 1966 and for over ten years now

Bhikkhu Anomandassi, a monk, has been giving courses in Buddhist studies so that students may understand Buddhist tenets, customs and culture. They are thus introduced to a knowledge of 'the other religions which are more widespread through individual areas. Thus, they can better understand the elements of goodness and truth which such religions possess by God's Providence . . .' (*Optatam Totius* 16).

Since Vatican II there has been a complementary theological training programme on a contextual level. Uva diocese, founded in 1973, has organized a Ministries' School. It yields a ministry of dialogue with Buddhists, and a ministry of dialogue with other religions, the two *sevakas* (meaning servantship, ministry) being engaged in a useful study of principles of dialogue, languages (Pali, Arabic, Sanskrit), to be dialogists for the diocese. Since 3 January 1975, this ministries' school has celebrated annually, three festivals, Thai Pongal—a harvest festival, with the Hindus, Milad-un-Nabi—the holy Prophet Muhammad's birthday—with Muslims, and Vesak day, a triple Buddhist festival recalling the birth, the enlightenment and the passing-away of the Buddha. Let our Buddhist dialogist speak: 'By far the most important feast of Dialogue was on Vesak day. At the town hall, three hundred people gathered in 1975 with a Christian chairman and with Hindu, Muslim, and Christian speakers greeting and feasting their Buddhist brethren on this all-important festival. The Venerable Amarakongana Amarawansa, monk of the Diyatalawa training school for monks said: "Till today, one would have thought that the Buddha Jayanthi of some years ago was the climax of it all. Today, we find we have gone further in a Dhamma Jayanthi where doctrines of truthfulness get together to feast Buddhism. It is a signal victory for religion".[4] The following year the Vesak festival was held with a delegation from the Congress of Religions'.[5]

All this reveals the process of dialogue in a land which is the cradle of Theravāda Buddhism. The Spirit of God has surely been moving in this direction for many years. If Christ is the *Dabar,* the Active Word or Speaking Action, then contemplation and action, reflexion-action in *praxis* are not departmentalized but convergent. He who inspired word and conclusion in the Council, also inspired activity in areas ripe for dialogue. A significant contribution to dialogue comes from the Centre for Religion and Society at Havelock Road, Colombo, whose director, Dr Lynn de Silva, a Methodist minister, began it in 1963. Its review, *Dialogue,* said in September 1963: 'The purpose of this bulletin is implied in its title and indicated in the editorial. Briefly, it is to foster among Christians an adequate and sympathetic understanding of Buddhism with a view to entering into creative dialogue with our

Buddhist friends. With this in view the Christian Institute of Buddhist Studies (CIBS) has been established under the sponsorship of the National Christian Council of Ceylon'. In 1974, changing its name to the Study Centre for Religion and Society, it re-oriented itself in a new series. Methodist Christianity is here an instrument of the Spirit to show the way practically to other Christian churches, in an upsurge of unity in community through dialogue. Its present scope is to foster an understanding of multilateral and bilateral dialogue without detriment to the authenticity of each religion.[6]

THE NEED TO CONTINUE; THE NEED TO CONFIRM

Two basic failures indicate two basic needs for the future: to *continue* dialogue as an essential part of our mission to people, and to *confirm* and strengthen those engaged in dialogue, without which our hope is not active. A pre-synodal survey under Canon Houtart of Louvain revealed: 35% considering the Buddhist revival as good, 27% condemning it; 13% receiving it with mixed feelings and 29% not knowing what it meant. Furthermore, 59.2% of the people wanted dialogue with Non-Christians (53% in rural areas and 61.4% in urban areas). For the great majority of people, the fact of being a Catholic does not in any way hinder social life. Social relationships with Buddhists must therefore be considered normal. But the synodal conclusions were not followed up. The Catholic newspaper, the *Messenger*, does not carry the middle-page spread it used to carry for festivals of other religions. The women religious in Colombo, from 1973-74, held up to thirty-five seminars on inter-faith dialogue, some being attended by as many as 110 Sisters, as at Holy Family Convent, Bambalapitiya, Colombo. The inter-faith group of higher-form students at a Good Shepherd convent school (St Bridget's) in 1970 ended the same year. The sisters' seminars stopped suddenly. The non-Christian news bulletin (mimeographed) begun at Archbishop's House, Colombo, ended after its first or second volume in 1969. One recalls the *stanchezza dei buoni*, tiredness of the good people, once spoken of by Pope Pius XII. The male religious, especially the Oblates (OMI Fathers) held a seminar in Laos, as a result of their S-SE Asia link-up, and one on Buddhist-Christian Dialogue in Sri Lanka in July 1974, the latter with Asian delegates, including Fr Marcello Zago, OMI, of the Laotian Buddhist Studies and Dialogue Centre. This is certainly one way in which 'religious offer great assistance to the sacred hierarchy. With increasing demands of the apostolate, they can and should offer that assistance more every day' (*Christus Dominus*, 34).[7]

Why is encouragement so wanting? Historically, the Church has been concerned with fostering the piety of the faithful in a closed-in sacramental system. Where the tenets of Vatican II do not percolate to the people, dialogue easily evaporates. Theologically, dialogue is not yet understood as part of mission, so that the 'numbers game' of counting the faithful and of flaunting the census goes on with a doleful look at the 'eighteen per cent Christians' in the world. This happened until the Mission Sunday posters of 1975. Vagueness and confusion may result in the case of mixed marriages and disparity of cult: in theory, faith is seen as a free gift of God and the free assent of man; in reality, a subtle emphasis may be laid on 'changing the faith of the other party'. Fresh theological thinking should not be debarred from higher circles of church policy in the context of a quickly de-centralizing Rome. If our local church theology—in the local church and of the local church—is real and alive, our hope would be more real and more vital. Otherwise not much is to be hoped for from dialogue. More Christians will have to extend the hand of fellowship to their fellow countrymen as co-religionists, for religion is better than irreligion, and unless we seek basic religion (religiosity), alienation and isolationism will be the results. The Western fervour for ecumenism with other Christians, must be matched by our fervour for what they term wider ecumenism, but what we regard as more imperative as we seek the kingdom, in a land where religions, living faiths and ideologies live side-by-side, yearning for a pre-existence rather than a mere co-existence. What little continuity there is, and what little confirmation, seem to have yielded the dawn of reciprocity in dialogue.

BUDDHIST-CHRISTIAN AND CHRISTIAN-BUDDHIST: RECIPROCITY

Dr Bryan de Kretser of the Prithipura Homes for Handicapped Children, who wrote on 'Man in Buddhism and Christianity', once asked the present writer of these lines: 'Why are Christians so arrogant as to always extend the right hand of fellowship to the Buddhists?' What answer but that love—*agapé* or *mettā*—impels us to do so? Perhaps the taking up of the proffered hand is slow to those who still live in an atmosphere of 'conversions' rather than first of self-conversion. A Buddhist monk wrote to Dr Lynn de Silva: 'I see no common ground where we could meet . . . Christianity talks from heaven, Buddhism from earth'.[8] As recently as March 1977, we would hear such accusing voices among Christians: 'Dialogue is a problem for Christians. We had co-existence among the common people. Missionaries brought a new discord. The arrogant evangelism resulted in the Buddhist revival . . . what is now surfacing is the result of guilt feeling among Christians'.[9]

Dialogue is talking and listening alternately, not together; nor is it the summation of two monologues in a quantitative increase of volume. There is a glimmer of hope of reciprocity. The Venerable Hapugoda Dhammananda, missionary-emeritus from the Mahabodhi society with twenty-two years' experience in India, said at the second Sevaka Sevana Vesak festival: 'This is the first time I see this kind of multi-religious dialogue in Sri Lanka'. He has since contacted us to consider a possible study centre for Buddhist monks to dialogue with Christians and others.[10] Dr Gunapala Dharmasiri, lecturer in the department of philosophy at Peradeniya University, is another exponent of the pos-sibilities of dialogue.[11] By far the most thought-provoking approach is that of Dr Padmasiri de Silva, head of the department of philosophy at the same university.[12]

CONCLUSION: HOPES FOR THE FUTURE

Love defies straight-jacketing, and so the apparent aloofness of the official Christian Churches resulted in the real entry of spontaneous workers and groups into those areas of dialogue that thrive on spon-taneity and freedom. If today's dialogue is to mature tomorrow, we cannot rest at the dead-level of expertise or even the level of metaphys-ical cavils, technicality and casuistry, or the *abhidhanna* level, alone. 'Friendly discussion on religious matters with men of other faiths is by no means the right or privilege of only a few', said the guidelines of the OMI-sponsored dialogue with Buddhists in July 1974. Then our areas of liberating hope would be: **first**, schools, religious men and women, institutes, centres that would have to sustain their efforts at dialogue and steadily encourage new-comers in dialogue. In this process, moves towards the solution of the problem of language—*le langage* rather than *la langue*—including beliefs, customs, culture, are necessary. The **second** must be concomitant with the first: and that is dialogue not only in word but in action, as a natural process in a Third World country. This is the dialogue with all men of good will (Pope Paul VI, *Develop-ment of Peoples*, 83), a dialogue in action.[13] The rural masses of Asia look up and are not fed. Solidarity with other Christians today and with Christians of the past demands reconciliation, and this also is an ex-pression of dialogue. If salvation is indicated as necessary and wished for in Buddhism (*etena saccena suvatthi hotu*, as some discourses of the Buddha end: by this truthful word may there be salvation), then we are not far away from the dynamism of a healthy liberation movement where Christians help as reconcilers by being aware, and in awareness-building on conscientization, which is the killing of igno-rance (*avijjā*) and the moral urge to change self-defeating structures of society. Dr Padmasiri's 'value orientations' and 'nation building' take dialogue into the realm of action and real life. Dr Lynn de Silva's study-centre occasional bulletins as they treat of racism, oppression, the gap between the rich and the poor, the relationship between developed and developing nations, ecology and pollution bring dialogue into sharper focus.[14] When dialogue matures into action without losing the *Dhamma*, the hopes and dreams of twenty years of dialogue will be fulfilled, for dialogue is a two-way process, and liberation would become the end result of dialogue, from ignorance to wisdom, from self-emptying to fulfilment.

Notes

1. V. Tennekoon, *The Great Rebellion of 1818* (Colombo, 1970), p. xlii.

2. M. Rodrigo, *Report on an Approach to Non-Christians*, January (Duruthu, 1965), (mimeographed, unpublished material), 11 pp. National Seminary, Kandy.

3. *Nostra Aetate*, Vatican II, 2, para 2.

4. L. Ranasingme, 'Rethinking Ministries at the Service of Uva, From Rite to Reality', in *Sevaka Sevana* Bulletin II (1976), p. 90. Also Frederick Perera, ibid., p. 103.

5. The Congress of Religions in Sri Lanka has official status by Act of Parliament of 1970.

6. Other centres include: Tulana Research and Encounter Centre (Director, Fr Aloysius Pieris SJ); Centre for Society and Religion (Director, Fr S. T. Balasuriya, OMI).

Theses (dissertations) include: Antony Fernando, OMI, *Poverty in the Vinaya Pitaka;* M. Rodrigo, OMI, *'The Enlightenment of the Buddha,'* Gregorian University (Rome, 1959), 1963. *The Moral Passover from Self to Selflessness in Buddhism, Christianity, Islam, Hinduism* (Institut Catholique de Paris, 1973).

7. By episcopal statute, Laos and Cambodia have a *Bureau de la Conference episcopale pour le Bouddhisme,* under Fr Marcello Zago, OMI. Sri Lanka, has no official Secretariat for Buddhist-Christian or multi-lateral dialogue. The liturgical *Ordo* makes mention of feasts of other religions, an important step forward.

8. Dr Lynn de Silva, 'The Understanding and Goal of Dialogue', in *Dialogue,* Vol. IV, 1-2 (1977), pp. 3-8, esp., p. 4, quoting a Buddhist monk's letter.

9. C. D. E. Premawardhana, reporting on the consultation on 'Dialogue in Community' in *Dialogue,* Vol. IV, 1-2 (Jan.-Aug., 1977), pp. 32-34.

10. L. Ranasinghe, 'Rethinking Ministries, Rite to Reality', *Sevaka Sevana II,* p. 90.

11. Dr Gunapala Dharmasiri, 'Meaning of Religion in Sri Lanka Today', in *Dialogue,* Vol. II, 1, pp. 7-11.

12. Dr Padmasiri de Silva, 'The Basis for Seeking Community, a Buddhist Point of View', in *Dialogue,* Vol. IV, 1-2 (1977), pp. 9-16.

13. See Fr T. Balasuriya, *Logos*, Feb. 1977; M. Rodrigo, *Dialogue*, Vol. III, 2, pp. 62-67; Vol. IV, 1-2, pp. 17-26; Lynn de Silva, *Study Centre Occasional Bulletins;* Padmasiri de Silva, *Value Orientations and Nation Building;* Bandarawela Devananda, *Sevaka Sevana Bulletin* III (1977), pp. 209-14.

14. Similar papers are issued as Dossiers of the Centre for Society and Religion (Director, Fr T. Balasuriya, OMI); also in the *Logos* series, 1975-76.

Marcello Zago

Buddhist-Christian Dialogue in
South-East Asia

BURMA, CAMBODIA, Laos and Thailand are four countries of the
Indochina peninsula sharing common characteristics. Their culture is
basically Indian even though their ethnic substratum gives each country its own physiognomy. The official and majority religion is
Theravāda Buddhism but this is deeply marked by symbiosis with an-
cestral animism.[1] The Christian presence is very slight throughout
these countries, consisting only of minority groups often foreign in
origin, despite a missionary effort several centuries old.[2]

Contacts between Christians and Buddhists have not been lacking in
the past, particularly in the early days. In Thailand in the seventeenth
century, Jesuits such as Le Blanc, de la Breuille and du Bouchet 'made
a point of winning over the Thailanders and winning them over to them'
and they noted that 'with regard to customs and the manner of leading
their lives, a Christian could not teach anything more perfect than what
their religion prescribed in this respect'.[3] In Burma, Catholic bishops
of the seventeenth and eighteenth centuries such as Percoto, Mon-
tegazza and Bigandet have left us numerous treatises on the customs
and rules of Buddhism.[4] In Cambodia, Fr Maldonado sought to 'assimi-
late himself as much as possible to the yellow-robed Bonzes in order to
sow the saving seed in the very interior of Buddhist monasteries'.[5]

The missionaries, despite their sincere sympathy for the culture and
socio-philosophical systems and above all for the peoples among whom
they lived, did not succeed either in developing an objective sympathetic view of Buddhism,[6] or in establishing a deep dialogue with the
Buddhists. They were hindered not only by the prejudices of their time

but above all by the theological approach which regarded other religions as human distortions and tricks of the devil. Colonization added to the difficulties standing in the way of mutual comprehension, even though the system of Catholic schools, especially in Thailand, favoured mutual respect among individuals.

Since independence, several factors have favoured new relationships between Christians and Buddhists. For example, the Christians have come out of their village ghettos and joined the process of urbanization; there is a need for collaboration on the social level, there are international and inter-religious meetings and finally, there is a new view of other religions, particularly among Catholics since Vatican II.

BURMA

Burma is the country where experience of dialogue seems weakest. A member of the Roman Secretariat for Non-Christian Religions, following a rapid visit to evaluate the situation, summed up his impressions like this: 'but as far as I can judge dialogue as such does not exist in Burma. This is due to numerous reasons, particularly the political tension'.

There is undoubtedly something being done in this direction, as the studies by Pasquale Anatriello[7] and Winston L. King[8] show, but dialogue has not been sought either by the religious authorities or the simple faithful. Memories of English colonization, the struggle—whose success was only ephemeral—to make Buddhism the State religion, the attitude of the present socialist and lay Government, have prevented Buddhists from taking the initiative in this direction. The Christians for their part originally felt themselves attacked by the Buddhist claims, then lost the majority of the foreign missionaries, which obliged those ministers who remained to concentrate their activity on service of the Christian communities, which were to be found mainly among non-Buddhist ethnic groups. The lack of contact with the outside world and the small number of native ministers made efforts at dialogue still more difficult.

CAMBODIA

The experience of Christian-Buddhist dialogue in the Khmer land was short. It happened between 1970 and 1975. Before this date any true meeting was virtually impossible despite the attempts of pastors such as Mgr Ramousse and Mgr Tep Im. The majority of Christians were and felt themselves to be foreigners. After the *coup d'état* of March 1970, only three or four thousand Catholics of the original seventy thousand remained in the country; the others departed for Viet-nam or were rounded up in camps for foreigners. Those who were left, finding themselves alone and deprived of their own social structures, in particular their schools, felt themselves obliged and encouraged to enter into dialogue with their Buddhist compatriots.

Besides individual dialogue, into which they were progressively initiated by special sessions as well as the ordinary course of pastoral work, the Christians in the towns took part in the relief work for refugees whose number constantly increased as a result of the war. This charitable work brought increasing contact with the Civil and Buddhist authorities. Other contacts between Christians and lay Buddhists were organized with the aim of developing mutual understanding; seminars and colloquies have taken place at Phnom-Penh and elsewhere.[9]

The presence of Benedictine monks has long been a favourable and encouraging element. The monastery at Kep had long been a house of prayer somewhat outside Buddhist monastic experience, as was the Carmelite convent at Phnom-Penh. The war brought about contact between Catholic monks and Buddhists. Several bonzes sought refuge in the monastery and young Buddhists joined the community, not in order to become Christians but to live a sort of religious life. The mutual influence has had a great effect not only on mutual understanding but on the process of adaptation. Buddhists came to regard the Christian monks as true religious and behaved towards them accordingly, organizing, for example, a traditional offering of habits (*Kathima*).

The 'liberation' of Phnom-Penh in April 1975 brought about the end of all religious structures, both Christian and Buddhist. The absolute equality imposed by the new authorities still prevents any form of monastic life, places obstacles in the way of all religious practice and has cut short all institutional dialogue. Manual work in the jungle, continual uprootings, sessions of political indoctrination and the suffering they have endured together are submitting all Khmers to the same common destiny.

LAOS

Laos is undoubtedly the country in which dialogue, better planned and benefiting from more sustained encouragement, has reached members of both religions in greatest numbers, both among the authorities and among the simple faithful, and this has even become a source of inspiration in neighbouring countries.[10] Thanks to a National Office and to diocesan authorities brought about and supported by the Conference of Bishops, all pastoral ministers (priests, religious and catechists) have been helped to renew both their outlook and their own efforts. Meetings between Christians and Buddhists on a friendly level have become more numerous, leading to mutual understanding, a sharing of deep experiences and practical collaboration. Researches on the experience of Buddhism have gone ahead and investigations have been carried out into particular problems such as the concept of deity among various groups, Christian and Buddhist ethics, and religious language.[11] This dialogue has also had official aspects such as the visit paid to the Pope by a Buddhist delegation presided over by the Patriarch of Laos in person.[12]

The depth and sincerity of dialogue was shown when the foreign missionaries were expelled from Louang-Prabang in August 1975. The Buddhist Patriarch did everything in his power to change the decision made by the party leaders, without however succeeding; he then showed the Buddhist attitude by organizing a solemn farewell ceremony in his monastery and by accompanying the missionaries to the airport. The anti-religious measures which the Government is taking to an ever-increasing degree against both Christians and Buddhists have not extinguished all the beneficial marks of the dialogue. If prayer meetings for small Christian groups are still allowed in some towns, this is probably due to the sympathy felt for them by the Buddhist population as a result of dialogue.

THAILAND

The outlook for dialogue in Thailand is positive even if, at present, the situation is stagnant despite the remarkable efforts of certain pioneers. The Catholic schools, which are populated mainly by Buddhists, had prepared the ground and men's minds.

Here, unlike in the other countries, the Buddhists took the initiative.[13] In 1958 the Buddhist University of Bangkok asked the bishop to appoint a Professor of Christian Religion. In the following years the Director General of the Department of Religions, Colonel Pin Mathukan, organized a joint day for the religions to meet and explain themselves to each and installed a permanent exhibition of religions in a room at the Ministry of Education. The outstanding bonze of the country, Buddhadâsa, also became interested in Christianity and this fact had a positive influence on Buddhists.[14] The Patriarch of Thailand paid a visit to the Pope in 1972.

The Protestants, who have generally been more reluctant to enter into dialogue and whose uncompromising stand on various points and methods has often raised obstacles, have here played a remarkable rôle thanks to the annual 'Sinclair Thompson Memorial' lectures at the Theological Seminary of Chieng-Mai.[15]

Some Catholics have carried the dialogue forward simply by their good human relations. One can point to Mgr Carretto and in particular to Fr John Ulliana, who has become one of the best-known and most influential figures in the national meetings organized by the Department of Religion, as well as in the social work of the co-operatives. Others such as Fr Pezet have contributed a deeper understanding of Buddhism through living for many years in Buddhist monasteries and practising meditation in a specialized centre.[16]

At present neighbourly relations are good: each religion invites members of the others to its feasts and religious ceremonies; there is mutual recognition and all expressions of disdain have vanished; the two religions work together on social projects, though dialogue often remains superficial due to a lack of effort at deep understanding often justified by motives of caution. Yet the country still presents a unique possibility, thanks to the quality of Thai Buddhism and because of the rôle it plays in other Buddhist countries.

CONCLUSION

Dialogue with Buddhists takes place on various levels. There is collaboration in social work, there are doctrinal exchanges, there is mutual exchange of information on practice and beliefs, there is a common setting of religious experiences; the level of contact usually depends on the interest and background of those taking part.

From the Christian side, the initiative has been taken by foreign missionaries; native ministers have followed the movement often with astonishment and usually with a great deal of prudence. The Roman Secretariat for Non-Christian Religions has helped progress along this road thanks to visits by the Secretary[17] and the general climate of encouragement given. Protestants have hardly begun to take an interest, with the exception of the Theological Seminary of Chieng-Mai; certain sects have rather hindered the efforts of other Christians by their attitudes. There is still a long road to be travelled before all Christians have a common attitude to dialogue and bring their support to it.

The political circumstances of the different countries play an important part. The Communist régimes in Cambodia and Laos with their anti-religious outlook make not only dialogue difficult, but even the survival of these religions, faced with the greatest challenge in their history: how to continue to be a grain of salvation and progress in spite of the decimation of their structures and in spite of persecution.

For Christianity dialogue is the essential condition for a real presence in Asia.[18] Without dialogue, there will be no incarnation, no intelligible re-expression of the message and above all, no real, meaningful and inviting growth.

Translated by Paul Burns

Notes

1. For an up-to-date description of Buddhism in these countries, see D. K. Swearer, 'Recent Developments in Thai Buddhism', in Dumoulin, *Buddhism in the Modern World* (London, 1967), pp. 99-108; W. L. King, 'Contemporary Burmese Buddhism', ibid., pp. 81-98; M. Zago, 'Contemporary Khmer Buddhism', ibid., pp. 109-19; idem., 'Buddhism in Contemporary Laos', ibid., pp. 120-29.

2. In Burma and Cambodia, the first missionary contacts go back to the mid-sixteenth century, with a continuous missionary presence from the middle of the eighteenth century. In Thailand, missionaries have been present since 1662. In Laos, though Fr Leiria stayed from 1642-47, there was no regular missionary presence till the late nineteenth century. In all these countries, the Christian population makes up less than one per cent of the total.

3. H. de Lubac, *Le rencontre du bouddhisme et de l'Occident* (Paris, 1952), pp. 92-93.

4. P. Anatriello, *Buddismo Birmano* (Naples, 1969), pp. 115-26.

5. H. de Lubac, op. cit., p. 93.

6. Cf. H. Trager, *Burma through Alien Eyes. Missionary Views of the Burmese in the Nineteenth Century* (New York, 1966); P. Phichit, 'My Visit to Burma', in *Bulletin Secretarius pro non christianis* XI/1 (1976), p. 66.

7. P. Anatriello, op. cit., pp. 127-43.

8. W. King, *Buddhism and Christianity. Some Bridges of Understanding* (London, 1962).

9. M. Zago, 'Visite aux confrères du Cambodge', in *Bull. Sec. pro non christianis* VII/2 (1972), pp. 71-76.

10. Idem. 'Le dialogue avec les bouddhistes au Laos', in ibid. X/2 (1975), pp. 277-91.

11. Of several duplicated studies on these and similar questions, some have since been published in books or reviews, e.g., M. Zago, 'L'équivalent de Dieu dans le bouddhisme', in *Eglise et Théologie* VI (1975), pp. 25-49, 153-74, 297-317; idem, 'Proclamation of the Kerygma to the Buddhists', in *Worldmission* 28/1 (1977), pp. 20-25.

12. Idem, 'The Visit of the Lao Buddhist Patriarch to Rome and Italy', in *Bull. Sec. pro non christianis* (1973), pp. 90-101.

13. P. Carretto, 'Dialogue between Christians and Buddhists in Thailand', in ibid. IX/3 (1974), pp. 209-13; P. Phichit, 'Dialogue Situation in Thailand', ibid. X/2 (1975), pp. 269-76; P. Rossano, 'Report on Mons. Rossano's Journey in S.E. Asia', ibid. XI/1 (1976), pp. 46-61.

14. Buddhadâsa makes frequent reference to Christian teaching and practice, which he often interprets in his own way. His best-known work is *Christianity and Buddhism* (Sinclair Thompson Memorial Lecture, Bangkok, 1967).

15. These lectures are designed to further mutual understanding between Christians and Buddhists in Thailand, through a series of specialized studies, published annually.

16. E. Pezet, 'Reflections on My Personal Experience in a Buddhist Country', in *Bull. Sec. pro non christianis* IX/3 (1974), pp. 176-85.

17. Reports appear regularly in the Bulletin of the Secretariat.

18. M. Zago, 'Présence du christianisme en Orient et dialogue', in *Kerygma* 7 (1973), pp. 147-72.

Hugo Enomiya-Lassalle

Buddhist-Christian Dialogue in Japan

INTRODUCTION

THE FIRST thing that has to be said in the context of this article is that Japanese Buddhism is never completely separate from Shintoism, the primitive religion that was at one time the state religion. In an enquiry a few years ago, an estimated forty million Japanese declared themselves to be adherents of both Shintoism and Buddhism. This certainly has nothing to do with nationalism nowadays, but reflects a very old religious usage that is still alive in Japan. As far as Buddhism is concerned, there are, in addition to the early sects that have been established in the country for centuries, countless more recent sects which cannot all be treated as alike. Unfortunately it is not possible to discuss each of these earlier and later sects in detail here.

As far as dialogue with Buddhism is concerned, a change in relationships between the religions of Japan took place soon after the end of the second World War. They came closer together, but did not take part in mutual consultations and made no explicit decisions. One striking symbol of the new relationships is that, from the very beginning, the anniversary of the dropping of the atomic bomb on Hiroshima (6 August) was commemorated not only officially by the city itself, but by Buddhists, Shintoists and Christians, who have annually held a communal hour of prayer at the burial place of those who died as a result of this terrible explosion.

Another purely religious phenomenon was the foundation of an association of Zen Buddhist monks and Catholic priests with the aim of improving religious understanding. The main activity of this association is the holding of meetings attended by members of both religions to hear a lecture by a Zen monk and another by a Catholic priest.

A little later, dialogue between Buddhists and Christians was given a great impetus by the decisions made at the second Vatican Council about relationships between the Church and other religions. The missionary activity of the Church was put in an entirely new light by the Decree *Ad gentes*.

THE DIALOGUE ITSELF

Since the second Vatican Council, not only Christians but representatives of Buddhism in Japan have actively sought dialogue, although this search did not begin with Vatican II. Dialogue has been sought to a far greater degree and indeed almost exclusively by the leaders of both religions, since the ordinary believers are in both cases not very advanced in understanding. In this respect, the situation is very different to that in Europe or the United States of America, for example, where many former Christians have looked to Buddhism in particular for a substitute, hoping to find in the eastern religion what they have failed to find in their own. In Japan, on the other hand, the representatives of dialogue on both sides have to be very careful to prevent any misunderstanding among those members of their own religion who have not grasped the real meaning of this dialogue. That is, after all, hardly surprising in view of the fact that the great body of believers, both Christian and Buddhist, have been educated for centuries in diametrically opposed directions.

Nonetheless, we in Japan are in various ways in dialogue with each other, if only as individuals and groups. What is more, the papal internuncio in Tokyo has helped our efforts considerably by arranging for the heads of the Buddhist sects to be invited again and again to our meetings. Christian experts have always been present at these meetings with Buddhist leaders so that discussion has been able to develop. At the conclusion of this discussion there has usually been a friendly meal. Individual and group discussion has also taken place, but it is not yet possible to have a comprehensive view of the whole. I shall therefore confine myself to a consideration of two groups with whose activities I am very familiar.

The first of these groups met for the first time ten years ago, and since that first meeting its members have come together every year for a few days to talk about a previously arranged theme. It is not an official association with statutes and contributions. It has always been a circle of friends consisting of Zen Buddhists, Protestant and Catholic Christians, Japanese nationals and foreigners. The first stimulus came from Dr Douglas Steere, a leading Quaker in the United States. He visited leading masters of Zen, who agreed to collaborate and joined the circle. Dr Steere confined himself to representatives of Zen Buddhism, because he was aware of the danger of the discussion becoming a debate between individual sects if representatives of those sects had been invited and this would have resulted in the original aim of the group being lost. Every year, when the group met, the suggestion has been made that at least part of the dialogue should be published and this hope was fulfilled for the first time this year. Publication, however, has never, since the group first began to meet, been the main purpose. What we have all had first and foremost in mind has always been an open exchange of ideas. We have always regarded the best aspect of our meetings together to be our gradually deepening knowledge and trust of each other and the fact that everyone is able to express his own view openly without having to fear that he might give offence. In the course of the group's existence, many members have had to leave and others have taken their places. At present there are forty-two members; with a few exceptions, they are all Japanese.

The second group is quite different to the first. Its task could be described as preparation for dialogue rather than dialogue itself. It does not, moreover, confine itself to Zen Buddhism, but includes other kinds of Buddhism. It calls itself the Ecumenical Group for the Study of Interfaith Dialogue and its members are Protestant and Catholic Christians. It is working to complete a three-year plan, the theme of the first year being historical investigation and assessment, that of the second year the theological implications of Buddhist-Christian dialogue and that of the third year the assessment of Buddhism. Buddhists who are interested in this dialogue are to be invited to take part in the theme of the third year. On the completion of the three-year plan, the group will consider the theme of a 'search for new guide-lines'.

DIFFICULTIES IN DIALOGUE WITH BUDDHISTS IN JAPAN

I shall not deal in this section with theological difficulties, as these are discussed in another article, but with two obstacles to dialogue that have shown themselves to be particularly hard to surmount. Both are of a practical nature.

The first is that both Christians and Buddhists have insufficient knowledge of each other's religion. Seen from the point of view of the Buddhists, Christians clearly have far too little understanding of Buddhism to be able to participate in fruitful dialogue. Conversations with Buddhists may well help Christians to learn more about the Buddhist religion, but the real theme of the debate remains untouched. It is, moreover, even more difficult for foreign Christians than for the Japanese to make up for a defective knowledge of Buddhism. In addition, there are many different sects, all of which have the same central teaching of illumination, but which differ, sometimes widely, in their interpretation of it. Even a fairly superficial knowledge of all these sects requires thorough study. There is also the difficulty of language. Translations from Chinese and Japanese are always inaccurate. The exactly corresponding words often do not exist in European languages and there is always a risk that the original terms may be placed in categories in the European language in question that do not exist in Japanese. For example, how should a Zen kōan, an insoluble problem given to a Zen disciple by his master, be translated into a European language? Zen masters therefore advise their European students to learn at least enough Japanese to be able to understand these texts after the meaning has been explained to them. This linguistic difficulty, of course, is not encountered in dialogue between Protestants and Catholics. The same applies, perhaps to an even greater degree, to the second of the two difficulties, which I shall now discuss briefly.

This difficulty is even more resistant to a solution than the first. It cannot, for example, be solved even if the partners in dialogue all know good Japanese. This is because the experience of illumination in Zen Buddhism cannot be expressed in words. The writings of the Zen master Dogen, the founder of the Japanese Soto sect, for example, cannot be perfectly understood if the 'eye of illumination' has not to some degree been opened. After exchanging a few words with a partner in dialogue, an illuminated Zen master will know whether the other is 'seeing' or not in this sense. The same applies to the writings of important Buddhist scholars. Anyone who is practically and not simply theoretically involved with Zen will soon realize that there is a real need for this experience in dialogue with Zen Buddhism if the conversations are ever to get off the ground. This does not mean, of course, that the master of Zen is unable to speak about his religion at the rational level. This is something that he would certainly have been trained to do. What it does mean, however, is that dialogue at this level is in the long run not really interesting for him. I am bound to add that this illumination or enlightenment does not necessarily have to be Zen illumination in the narrower sense. (This name is really incorrect, since the experience is purely one of illumination and cannot be qualified in any way.) In other words, the experience could also be that of the Christian mystic and many masters of Zen have some knowledge of the Christian mystics and feel that an encounter with them would be fruitful.

I have spoken so far about Christians' lack of knowledge of Buddhism. There is also the difficulty that arises in dialogue because of the Buddhists' faulty knowledge of the Christian religion. There are, of course, exceptions. There are Zen masters who read Scripture and value it highly. But, as far as Christian teaching is concerned, most

Buddhists assume a knowledge of it, not only among Christians generally, but among theologians, that is nowadays completely superseded
and that would in the West be regarded as rudimentary even for small
children. One is often astonished by statements made by Buddhists
about the 'Christian' view of God—a view which the Christian himself
would apply to an idol. This is very regrettable and is a great obstacle
for the Zen Buddhist in any attempt to come closer to Christianity and
participate in dialogue with Christians.

The language of Scripture is, of course, based on a world-view that
was suitable for men of that time but is now superseded. The Zen
Buddhist, however, is extremely susceptible here. He does not recognize the existence of a positive way of expressing the Absolute. He
prefers to call it the Nothing or the Void. The early masters of Zen had
a saying: 'As soon as you open your mouth, you have already fallen
into a thousand errors'.

Fortunately, there are many deeply-convinced Christians who practise Zen. Some of them have already experienced illumination, having
been led to this by a Zen master. These Christians can make a very
important contribution to the dialogue with Zen Buddhism.

Finally, an important comment. There is a dialogue that takes place
with words. It can only be expressed in words. But there is also a
dialogue that takes place in action. It is a risky venture into the other
religion—an experience that Thomas Merton risked. Many other Christians have in this way become, as it were, 'Buddhists'. The Benedictine
Le Saux followed this way in India and had the 'great experience' of
Buddhism before he died. This was, of course, an exceptional and
special vocation. But we should thank God that such vocations exist.

Translated by David Smith

Joseph Spae

The Influence of Buddhism in Europe and America

AS THE western world of our convictions shakes under our feet an emptiness is left behind from which generations try to escape into artificial life-styles, exotic doctrines, and utopias. The true as well as the imagined Buddhism helps to fill this vacuum. Where and how do we hear its voice?

The 'western emptiness' appears to some as the negation of the Christian pleroma in a triple sphere: 1. a breakdown of traditional values under the trauma of pluralism and the burden of excessive choice; 2. disillusionment with the gaping contradiction between profession and performance; 3. the seeming irrelevance of Christianity to solving the crisis.

Hence the 'Buddhist emptiness' (the Sanskrit *sūnyatā*), the basic ideal on which all major schools agree, fascinates the western subconscious: 1. It lays claim to a holistic view of human personality which unites intellect and will, balances thought and action, and integrates intellectual profundity with spiritual discipline; 2. it puts man squarely within, and not over, nature; 3. it fosters a meditative way of life resistant to consumer greed. All this is some promise of a new age of justice and peace.

The appeal of Buddhism and its challenge to Christianity are not limited to a few million people in our subcultures. The Buddhist-Christian influence is mutual and universal. Here I am concerned with one aspect of this mutuality: the creative tension between Buddhism and theology in the West.

MINI-SOCIOLOGY

Although the Buddhist influence is without frontiers, it has cultural contours. The number of active Buddhist groups in the West has increased sharply since the nineteen-sixties. It now stands at about four hundred. In order of importance, these groups are active in the USA, Germany and England. They publish about fifty, mostly popular, periodicals. These add their weight to a great number of publications, edited in the East but also valued in the West, such as the scholarly *Eastern Buddhist* (Kyoto) and the informative *World Buddhism* (Colombo).

Statistics of group membership are vague. In terms of influence, I distinguish between people who made a formal commitment to Buddhism through taking the Three Refuges, a kind of religious profession which expresses trust in Buddha, his doctrine and his community; listed members of Buddhist churches; and people who occasionally engage in some Buddhist practice such as sutra chanting or meditation. Layman puts the total number of these people at half a million, of whom ninety per cent live on the West Coast. There might be about 50,000 in the first category, 300,000 in the second, and 150,000 in the third. In Europe, perhaps as many as 100,000 people claim some Buddhist interest or affiliation. Thus the German Buddhist Union (Deutsche Buddhistische Union), founded in 1958, lists close to three thousand members. According to Mildenberger, thousands of German Christians have followed Zen-inspired meditation courses in famous monasteries such as Beuron and Maria Laach, and more than 20,000 meditate daily according to its rules. The number of meditation groups and centres under Christian auspices has increased annually, particularly in America. Harvey Cox describes life at Weston Priory, Vermont, and wittily remarks that 'the Tibetans are, in some sense, the Benedictines of Buddhism'.

The composition of recent Buddhist groups is probably much the same as that of other groups advocating eastern religions. Devotees are usually affluent, well-educated, politically liberal, white and fairly young; their median age is close to twenty-two years and about five per cent are over thirty. This means that many are in the basic process of changing their lives. As to their religious background, if statistics relating to the Hare Krishna movement in the USA apply to them, the parents' religious affiliation would indicate that eighteen per cent come from Catholic, thirteen per cent from Methodist, and fourteen and a half per cent from Jewish homes, whereas twenty-five per cent grew up in non-denominational surroundings. In Europe one gains the impression that the number of younger Buddhist devotees is on the wane while that of serious searchers for Buddhist insights of interest to Christianity is growing fast. This fact explains a deepening influence of Buddhism in the theological field that calls for more advanced studies and further contacts.

NOMENCLATURE

It is common knowledge that the futurology of Western civilization betrayed Buddhist overtones from Schopenhauer (1788-1860) to Spengler (1880-1936). Schopenhauer in turn influenced Wagner's (1813-1883) *Tristan und Isolde,* and both left tell-tale marks on Nietzsche's (1844-1900) *Übermensch.* Hesse's *Siddhartha* (1922) reached an eighth Dutch edition in 1973. Babbitt's English translation (1936) of the *Dhammapada,* an early Buddhist devotional book, influenced Walter Lippmann, David Riesman and T. S. Eliot. The list of similar influences is very long.

More important to our theme is a plethora of Christian theologians who have come to grips with the challenge of Buddhist thought. In the forefront of recent scholarly research, which is also of theological significance, we find two Catholics, L. de la Vallée Poussin and his famous disciple E. Lamotte. Their joint opus is a *summa buddhologica* which professional theologians dare not overlook.

Among the contributors to a comparative Buddhist-Christian theology are T. Altizer, K. Barth, E. Benz, T. Berry, R. Corless, J.-A. Cuttat, J. Lopez-Gay, D. T. Niles, I. Quiles, K. L. Reichelt, P. Rossano, P. Tillich, H. Waldenfels and S. Yagi. Systematic if fragmentary 'Buddhism-and-Christianity' books have been written by T. Callaway, E. Cornelis, R. Drummond, J. Masson, F. Masutani, Y. Raguin and G. Siegmund. Zen, whose influence seeps deeper into the Christian consciousness than that of any other Buddhist school, is drawing particular attention. D. T. Suzuki (1870-1966), the prolific author and occasional critic of Christianity who introduced Zen to the West, remains unrivaled for breadth of scholarship and influence. But other scholars are vying for attention, such as M. Abe, H. Dumoulin, H. Enomiya-Lassalle, A. Graham, W. Johnston, T. Merton, K. Nishitani, K. Takizawa and A. Watts. There is a wide variety of recent doctoral theses on basic theological themes: G. Bond's *The Problem of Interpretation in Theravāda and Christianity,* J. Chuck's *Zen Buddhism and Paul Tillich: A Comparison of Their Views on Man's Predicament and Its Resolution,* J. Kim's *Daisetz T. Suzuki and Paul J. Tillich: A Comparative Study of Their Thoughts on Ethics in Relation to Being,* and M. Sumanashanta's *A Comparison of Buddhist and Christian Perfection.* Similar doctoral research is promoted at European and Asian universities. Finally, many well-known theologians such as H. Kūng in *On Being a Christian* (New York, 1976) and E. Schillebeeckx in *Gerechtigheid en liefde, genade en bevrijding* (Brugge 1977), risk brief but interesting comparisons between doctrinal points in Buddhism and Christianity. Small wonder that the quantity and quality of publications related to my theme has grown immensely. I would refer the reader to some two hundred titles catalogued in my *The Buddhist-Christian Encounter* (1977).

TYPOLOGY

Romano Guardini's premonition to the effect that Buddhism might well become the last great challenge to Christianity finds support in the variety of themes in Buddhist-Christian encounter. They include doctrine (the nature of man and the self, the search for the historical Jesus and Buddha, God, faith and revelation, the Church and the Buddhist community), ethics (life-sustaining values, virtues and vices, Christian charity and Buddhist compassion), social concern (secularization, ecology, disarmament, Marxism *versus* Buddhism and Christianity), and above all spiritual experience (suffering and salvation, enlightenment and mysticism, prayer and contemplation).

Buddhist-Christian dialogue has invariably promoted greater Christian unity. Christian ecumenism becomes an incentive to Buddhist ecumenism. There is an increasing reciprocal empathy of the two religions. In Buddhist terms, we largely agree on the unsatisfactory nature of a world steeped in suffering, violence and frustration; on the need to transcend our predicament by emphasizing spiritual values; on society's basic responsibility for the humanization of life; on inner growth through purification and asceticism; and on man's eternal yearning for peace and salvation. Theravāda Buddhism and Catholic Christianity alike hold high the ideal of consecrated celibacy and monasticism, and efforts are being made to co-operate in this area; they are centred, on the Catholic side, on the Paris headquarters of the Benedictine Aide Inter-Monastères.

Buddhist-Christian parallels and incompatibilities surface at every encounter. The main, emotive incompatibility is Christ, seen by Christians as the universal saviour, upon whose redemptive action rests the final unity of all mankind. Many Buddhist scholars are aware of this doctrine. They want assurance that it does not imply the abolition of religious pluralism, either as a means of spreading the Christian faith or as a social ideal. They would be pleased if the Catholic Church proclaimed in their regard, perhaps in terms similar to those of the Venice Catholic-Jewish statement (30 March 1977), that it disavowed all efforts at conversion that were irreconcilable with human dignity and God's free gift of faith.

TOWARDS BUDDHIST-CHRISTIAN WHOLENESS

The Buddhist charism in relation to Christianity might well be that it enhances the sense of mystery and mysticism, illustrates the role of the guru or spiritual master, helps us to rediscover the body as an integral participant in man's ascent to God, and is a universal humanism. The Buddhist insistence on the centrality of religious experience and on the practice of piety in pursuit of salvation balances the excesses of intellectualism and legalism.

Christian theology takes note of all these points as dialogue travels a three-lane road from contrast, through convergence, to assumption. As yet we find more contrast than convergence, and the integration of elements borrowed from a Buddhist style of life for the sake of liturgical, catechetical and pastoral renewal remains a tantalizing theological task. This could lead to mutual enrichment, even to a new type of Buddhist-Christian wholeness and self-identification quietly or loudly demanded by pro-Orientalists. The success of this theological venture will be assured if Buddhists and Christians take seriously an intuition first suggested by St Thomas and later honoured by Vatican II in *Nostra Aetate,* 2, to the effect that 'the exchange of one's particular goods is the quintessence of charity' (*Summa Theologica,* 2-2, q. 138).

One can safely forecast that the influence of Buddhism in the West will increase. One danger threatening this influence is the possibility that Buddhism might become, in the few countries where it is still free, yet another 'civil religion', unable critically to evaluate Western values or unwilling to join forces with Christianity and eradicate the root causes of our suffering, the abuse of power and the violence of greed.

We all can agree with the German-born Lama Anagārika Govinda writing in the *Annual Journal* of the Tibetan Nyingma Meditation Center at Berkeley, California: 'We may hope that, when the followers of Christ and those of the Buddha meet again on the ground of mutual goodwill and understanding, there will come a day when the love which both Buddha and Christ preached so eloquently, will unite the world in the common effort to save humanity from destruction by leading it towards the Light in which we all believe' (*Crystal Mirror,* 1975, p. 242).

Dare we assume that one day Buddhism, with its blankness and beauty, its calm and charm, will cease to be a foreign body, and will make a fitting contribution to Christianity at the confluence of East and West? The period of passive waiting for an answer to this question is now at an end.[1]

Notes

1. A bibliographical note: H. Cox, *Turning East, the Promise and Peril of the New Orientalism* (New York, 1977); E. M. Layman, *Buddhism in America* (Chicago, 1976); M. Mildenberger, *Heil aus Asien? Hinduistische und buddhistische Bewegungen im Westen* (Stuttgart, 1974); J. Spae, *The Buddhist-Christian Encounter* (Brussels, 1977) (in five languages).

CONTRIBUTORS

ANDRE BAREAU was born at Saint'Mandé, France, in 1921. He was a research-worker at the National Centre for Scientific Research from 1947 to 1956, director of studies in Buddhist philology at the Ecole Pratique des Hautes Etudes, Paris, from 1956 to 1973. He has been professor in Buddhist studies at the Collège de France since 1971. He has published many works on Buddhism.

JAMES W. BOYD was born at Manitowoc, Wisconsin, USA, in 1934. He studied at Northwestern University and is now associate professor in the Department of Philosophy at Colorado State University. He has been a visiting associate professor in Iran. He has published many articles on Buddhism including studies of evil, Jainism and comparative studies of Christianity and Buddhism.

ROGER CORLESS was born at Wallasey, Cheshire, England, in 1938. He studied theology at King's College London and Buddhism at Wisconsin-Madison, USA, and studied later at Chicago, and in India and Japan. He is associate professor at Duke University, Durham, North Carolina, USA, and has published on Buddhism and Taoism.

DOMINIQUE DUBARLE, OP, was born at Biviers, Isère, France, in 1907. He became a Dominican in 1925. He studied theology and science in Paris. He has been professor of philosophy at the Saulchoir and professor of philosophy of science at the Institut Catholique de Paris. He has published on optimism, science and Christianity, theology of science, Hegel, and Marxism.

HEINRICH DUMOULIN was born in the Rhineland, Germany, in 1905. He was ordained in 1933. Since 1935 he has lived in Japan. He taught at Sophia University and since 1976 he has been professor emeritus of the University in religious science and the history of philosophy. He has published a history of Zen Buddhism and various studies of Buddhism.

MARIASUSAI DHAVAMONY, SJ, was ordained in Kurseon, India, in 1958. He is professor of Hinduism and of the history of religions at the Gregorian University, Rome. He is editor of *Studia Missionalia* and *Documenta Missionalia* and has written many books and articles.

HUGO ENOMIYA-LASSALLE, SJ, was born in Nieheim, Germany, in 1898. He studied in Germany, the Netherlands and Britain. He went to Japan in 1929. He taught at Sophia University and did missionary and social work. He has taught at Hiroshima University and since 1968 has worked at the Shinmeikutsu Zen Centre fifty miles from Tokyo. He has published many studies of Zen meditation and other aspects of Zen Buddhism.

MERVYN FERNANDO is secretary of the Commission for Dialogue with Non-Christians of the Sri Lanka Episcopal Conference. He is visiting lecturer in religion and psychology at the National Theological Seminary, Kandy, and at the Aquinas College of Higher Studies, Colombo. He has published articles on Buddhist-Christian themes in many journals.

MICHAEL RODRIGO was born in Dehiwela, Sri Lanka, in 1927. He was ordained in 1954. He studied at the Gregorian in Rome and at the Institut Catholique de Paris. He was professor of philosophy and liturgy at the National Seminary, Kandy, from 1955 to 1974 and is director of the Sevaka Sevana Ministries School and the Pastoral Kendra (Centre) of the new diocese of Uva.

MAHA STHAVIRA SANGHARAKSHITA is an Englishman who spent twenty years in the East studying and practising the three major historical forms of Buddhism. After the last war he settled in the Himalayan town of Kalimpong and remained there until 1964. He received the lower and higher ordinations in 1963-64. In 1957 he established the Triyana Vardhana Vihara, a centre of interdenominational Buddhism and became closely associated with the movement for the mass conversion of the Indian untouchables to Buddhism. He returned to England in 1964. He has lectured extensively on Buddhism and has published introductions to the subject.

JOSEPH SPAE was born in Lochristi, Belgium, in 1913. He studied at Leuven, Peking, Kyoto and Columbia University, New York. He went to China in 1937 and to Japan in 1938. He has specialized in relations between Christianity and Japanese culture. He founded a religious research institute in Tokyo in 1964 and was General Secretary of

SODEPAX. He has published more than a hundred articles and books on Christianity and Japan, Shintoism, and Sinology.

FRITS VOS was born at Delft, the Netherlands, in 1918. He teaches Japanese and Korean language and literature at the Rijks University in Leiden and is director of the Japanology Studies Centre there.

MARCELLO ZAGO was born at Treviso, Italy, in 1932. He was a missionary in Laos from 1959 to 1966 and from 1970 to 1975. He has published on Laotian Buddhist rites and ceremonies. He was guest professor in missiology at San Paolo University, Ottawa in 1968 and professor of missiology at the Lateran, Rome, in 1976. He has been a consultant to the Secretariat for Non-Christians since 1972.